ADA CARTIANU

AWAKENING OF A
Starseed

CONNECTING WITH YOUR STARSEED ENERGY
A PHILOSOPHICAL EXPLORATION

RebELLE Publishing Agency
Printed in the United States of America

AWAKENING OF A STARSEED
CONNECTING WITH YOUR STARSEED ENERGY
A PHILOSOPHICAL EXPLORATION

Our book may be purchased in bulk.
Please contact your local book seller, Barnes & Noble,
IngramSpark, Amazon, RebELLE P.A
or Ada Cartianu Art Gallery a
office@adacartianu.com
www.AdaCartianu.com

TABLE OF CONTENTS

*Doubt not the vastness within you, for
you carry the echoes of galaxies.
Your purpose is to awaken, and to remind
Earth of its own stardust origins.*

DEDICATION

To the countless Starseeds walking this Earth, whose unwavering spirits and sensitive hearts illuminate the path for us all. May this book serve as a beacon of understanding and support, guiding you towards the embrace of your unique gifts and the fulfillment of your cosmic purpose. This is dedicated to those who have felt the pull of the stars, the whisper of a forgotten home, the yearning for something more, a profound connection to the universe. Your journey is not solitary; you are woven into the fabric of existence, and your contributions are deeply valued. May this work help you find your voice, your power, and your rightful place in the grand cosmic symphony.

To those who have felt lost and alone, may this be a reminder that you are not alone, and that your unique path is crucial to the unfolding evolution of this reality. To those who have questioned, searched, and yearned, may this book be a testament to the power of self-discovery and the fulfillment of your divine destiny.

PREFACE

For many years, I journeyed through the landscapes of psychology and philosophy, seeking answers to the profound questions that haunted me. My own experiences, marked by heightened sensitivity and an inexplicable pull towards the universe, led me down an unexpected path, one that entwined the seemingly disparate worlds of science and spirituality. It was during this time, immersed in the study of human consciousness and the intricacies of the human psyche, that I encountered the concept of Starseeds. This belief system resonated deeply within me, offering a framework for understanding my own unique experiences and the experiences of many others who felt a similar sense of "otherness."

This book examines the Starseed belief system and discusses the potential impact of recognizing one's individual abilities, understanding energy dynamics, and engaging in the process of self-discovery.

I have gathered my knowledge acquired as an avid researcher to understand human nature, our profound desire to belong, my philosophical musings, and feelings to paint a picture of what it means to be a Starseed in this unprecedented global shift. I hope that the insights shared within these pages will resonate with you, illuminate your path, and empower you to embrace your own Starseed potential.

This is a guide to self-discovery, and a celebration of the unique and vital role each Starseed plays in shaping the future of our world.

May this work serve as a companion on your personal journey towards cosmic understanding and self-realization.

While this book draws upon extensive research and personal experiences, it is primarily a personal philosophical exploration. Further exploration into related topics can be pursued through research into New Age spirituality, transpersonal psychology, and related fields.

INTRODUCTION

Have you ever felt a profound sense of not quite belonging, a subtle disconnect from the world around you? Have you experienced heightened sensitivity, an almost overwhelming empathy for others, or vivid dreams filled with symbolic imagery and cosmic landscapes? If so, you may be one of the many individuals who resonate with the concept of being a Starseed—a soul originating from another planet or galaxy, here on Earth to fulfill a specific purpose. This book embarks on a journey into the fascinating world of Starseeds, exploring the compelling belief system that surrounds them and its implications for personal growth and spiritual transformation. We will delve into the core tenets of Starseed belief, exploring its origins and examining the common characteristics attributed to Starseeds.

We'll examine the challenges they often face: feelings of isolation, misunderstood sensitivities, difficulty fitting into conventional societal structures – and reframe these experiences as potent opportunities for self-discovery and growth. This book is more than just a theoretical exploration; it's a practical guide for navigating the complexities of being a Starseed in the 21st century. Through philosophical insights, and practical techniques, we will explore how to harness your unique energies, connect with universal energy, and discover your life purpose. We will explore the concepts of Indigo Children and Twin Flames, and how they relate to the Starseed experience. We will examine the role of suffering in personal growth and spiritual transcendence.

This is an invitation to embark on a profound journey of self-discovery, to embrace your unique gifts, and to understand your place within the grand cosmic design. The path ahead is one of self-acceptance, empowerment, and the fulfillment of your soul's purpose.

Prepare to embark on a journey of cosmic awakening and self-realization.

You are a constellation in human form, a gathering of starlight merged into a soul. Remember your celestial origins, and bring harmony to Earth.

UNDERSTANDING
The Starseed Concept

Have you ever looked up at the star-strewn sky and felt an inexplicable longing, a sense of belonging that transcends the boundaries of Earth? Have you ever felt different, an outsider looking in, even amongst those you love? If so, you may be hearing the faint but persistent echoes of your cosmic origins, stirring within you a profound awakening. This book is for you, the Starseed, the wanderer with stardust in your soul, yearning to remember who you truly are and the mission you came here to fulfill.

This is not a book of science fiction, nor is it a rejection of the beauty and wonder of our earthly home. Rather, it is an exploration of the potential for a deeper, more expansive understanding of our place in the universe, grounded in both spiritual wisdom and a philosophical quest for meaning. Prepare to embark on a journey of self-discovery, a journey that will unravel the mysteries of your soul and ignite the dormant potential that lies within.

Stars have been a source of fascination for humans since the dawn of time. They have been the subject of countless myths, legends, and stories, and have inspired countless poets, artists, and scientists. But what if stars were not just celestial bodies, but also containers of consciousness and wisdom? This is the idea behind the concept of Starseeds, souls who have had lives in other star systems, galaxies, and even dimensions, before incarnating on Earth.

The concept of Starseeds is not new, and can be traced back to various ancient traditions and spiritual teachings. However, it has gained renewed interest in recent times, as more and more people report experiencing a sense of otherworldly connection, and a deep inner knowing that they are not from this planet.

Starseeds are believed to be highly evolved souls, who have incarnated on Earth with a specific mission or purpose. They carry within them the wisdom, experiences, and unique perspectives of the far-off places they have come from, and are here to help raise the consciousness of humanity and assist in the evolution of the planet.

Starseeds often report feeling like outsiders, and may struggle to fit in with societal norms and expectations. They may have a deep sense of longing for something they can't quite put their finger on, and may feel a strong connection to the stars, the moon, and the cosmos. They may also have vivid dreams and memories of other worlds and dimensions, and may have a natural affinity for spirituality and metaphysical concepts.

One of the key characteristics of Starseeds is their deep sense of purpose and mission. They are here to help humanity shift from a fear-based consciousness to a love-based consciousness, and to assist in the creation of a new paradigm based on unity, cooperation, and harmony. They are often drawn to careers and activities that allow them to make a positive impact on the world, such as healing, teaching, and activism.

Another characteristic of Starseeds is their ability to access and channel higher frequencies of consciousness. They may have a natural ability to tap into their intuition and inner guidance, and may be able to access information and wisdom from other realms and dimensions. They may also have a strong connection to crystals, plants, and other forms of earth energy, and may be able to use these tools to help heal and balance the energy fields of others.

While the concept of Starseeds may seem far-fetched to some, there is a growing body of evidence to suggest that consciousness is not confined to the physical body, and that the soul is capable of traveling beyond the boundaries of time and space. Many people report having past-life memories and experiences, and there is a growing body of research on near-death experiences, which suggest that consciousness continues to exist after the physical body dies.

We know that throughout generations, the concept of "Starseed" has captivated the imaginations of many seeking a deeper understanding of their place in the universe. It's a belief system rooted in the idea that certain individuals possess souls originating from other planets or star systems, carrying with them unique characteristics and a profound sense of purpose on Earth. While not a scientifically proven concept, its resonance within New Age spirituality and metaphysical circles is undeniable, reflecting a growing interest in exploring non-traditional perspectives on human identity and the cosmos. Understanding the Starseed concept requires delving into its multifaceted nature, acknowledging its diverse interpretations, and tracing its roots through various spiritual and cultural traditions.

The term "Starseed" itself doesn't possess a singular, universally agreed-upon definition. Its meaning is fluid, evolving through interpretations within different spiritual communities and individual experiences. Some define Starseeds as souls who consciously chose to incarnate on Earth to assist in its evolution, acting as catalysts for positive change. Others view Starseeds as individuals carrying advanced spiritual knowledge and abilities, brought forth from other worlds to help humanity progress. Still others might associate the term with specific extraterrestrial races or civilizations, believing that Starseeds retain memories or genetic imprints from their origins. This lack of a rigid definition adds to the concept's intrigue, inviting personal interpretation and exploration.

The origins of the Starseed belief system are multifaceted, drawing from various ancient mythologies and modern spiritual movements. Ancient cultures across the globe—from the Sumerians with their tales of

Anunnaki to the Egyptians with their belief in divine beings descending from the heavens—often featured narratives of extraterrestrial visitors or beings with otherworldly origins impacting humanity's development. These stories, passed down through generations, laid the groundwork for modern interpretations of the Starseed concept.

The surge in interest in the Starseed concept in recent decades correlates with the rise of New Age spirituality. This movement, characterized by its emphasis on personal growth, self-discovery, and a holistic view of life, provides a fertile ground for exploring ideas that challenge conventional worldviews. The Starseed concept resonates particularly well with individuals who feel a sense of "otherness," a disconnect from mainstream society, or a deep longing for something beyond the mundane. It offers a framework for understanding these feelings, providing a sense of belonging and validation.

Differentiating the Starseed concept from similar concepts like "Lightworkers" and "Indigo Children" is crucial. While there's often overlap, subtle distinctions exist. Lightworkers are often considered individuals dedicated to bringing light and positive energy to the world, often through service and compassion. While many Starseeds may also identify as Lightworkers, the Starseed concept adds the layer of an interstellar origin. Indigo Children, on the other hand, are often characterized by their heightened intuition, creativity, and empathy, frequently seen as possessing a heightened sensitivity to energy. Again, there can be overlap, as many Starseeds may also exhibit Indigo traits, but the focus on past-life connections and extraterrestrial origins differentiates the core concept.

The historical and cultural context significantly impacts our understanding of the Starseed concept. The ancient myths and stories, though often metaphorical, highlight a persistent human fascination with the possibility of life beyond Earth and the potential influence of extraterrestrial beings on our evolution. These narratives provide a rich blend of symbolism and imagery that informs the modern interpretations of the Starseed concept, giving it depth and resonance. Modern New Age spirituality, with its focus on personal empowerment and spiritual exploration, provides a framework for integrating these ancient ideas into a contemporary context. The rise of UFOlogy and the growing acceptance of alternative perspectives in society also contribute to the popularity and broader acceptance of the Starseed belief system.

The concept of Starseeds also intertwines with the belief in past lives and reincarnation. Many who identify as Starseeds report experiences of past-life regression, vivid dreams, or spontaneous memories that suggest connections to other worlds or civilizations. These memories, though subjective and often difficult to verify, can offer significant emotional and spiritual insight, strengthening the belief in their extraterrestrial origins. Past-life regression therapy, a technique used to access and process memories from past lives, can be a powerful tool for uncovering and understanding these experiences. However, it's crucial to approach past-life regression with a critical and discerning mindset, understanding that these memories are deeply personal and may be symbolic or metaphorical.

The nuances associated with the term "Starseed" are numerous and complex. Some individuals identify as belonging to specific star systems, planets, or even extraterrestrial races, each associated with unique characteristics and energetic signatures. Others avoid such specific classifications, preferring a broader understanding of the concept. This diversity of interpretations highlights the personal and subjective nature of the Starseed experience. The term serves as a unifying label for individuals who share a common feeling of otherness, a heightened sensitivity, and a deep connection to the cosmos, even though their specific experiences and beliefs may vary considerably. The journey of understanding one's identity as a Starseed is often one of self-discovery and exploration, a process of integrating personal experiences with the broader belief system.

Understanding the complex nature of the Starseed concept requires an open mind and a willingness to explore both the tangible and intangible aspects of human experience. While the concept remains outside of the realm of conventional science, its resonance within spiritual and metaphysical communities is a testament to its power to help individuals understand their place in the universe and find meaning in their lives. The lack of a rigid definition allows for personal interpretation and exploration, making it a dynamic and evolving belief system that continues to inspire and resonate with many. As we continue to explore the mysteries of the cosmos and our place within it, the concept of Starseeds will undoubtedly continue to evolve and adapt, reflecting our ongoing quest for understanding. This initial exploration provides a foundational understanding of this intricate and compelling concept. The following chapters will delve deeper into the unique traits and challenges often associated with the Starseed experience, offering insights and guidance for those who resonate with this belief system.

The concept of Starseeds offers a fascinating and intriguing perspective on the nature of the soul and the purpose of life on Earth. Whether or not you believe in the literal existence of souls from other star systems, the idea that we are all connected, and that we carry within us the wisdom and experiences of countless lifetimes, is a powerful and empowering one. By embracing our inner Starseed, we can tap into our highest potential, and help create a world that is based on love, unity, and harmony.

THE CALL TO EARTH
Starseeds and the Evolutionary Imperative

The "Starseeds," souls believed to have originated from other star systems and planetary civilizations, choosing to incarnate on Earth is a compelling and increasingly popular notion. It suggests a cosmic imperative, a profound desire to contribute in the planet's evolution, particularly during critical junctures of transformation. These incarnations, it is argued, are not random occurrences but rather conscious decisions driven by a yearning to raise consciousness, heal the planet, and usher in a new era of peace and harmony. Examining the reasons why Starseeds choose to answer this "Call to Earth" reveals a complex design of karmic responsibility, spiritual purpose, and profound empathy for the human experience.

One of the primary drivers behind a Starseed's decision to incarnate on Earth is the desire to assist in raising planetary consciousness. Earth, in its current state, is often perceived as a planet grappling with duality, negativity, and disconnection. Starseeds, possessing a higher vibrational frequency and a broader perspective gained from their extraterrestrial origins, are believed to be equipped to introduce new paradigms of thought and being.

Their inherent understanding of interconnectedness, empathy, and unconditional love serves as a catalyst for shifting the collective consciousness towards a more positive and unified state.

By embodying these qualities in their daily lives, they act as guides, inspiring others to question existing norms, embrace their own spiritual potential, and contribute to a more enlightened world. This raising of consciousness is not a passive endeavor; it requires active participation in dismantling outdated systems and promoting philosophies that prioritize compassion, sustainability, and unity.

Also, the call to Earth is often deeply intertwined with a profound desire to heal the planet. Earth faces unprecedented environmental challenges, driven by human activity and a disregard for the natural world. Starseeds, often possessing a profound connection to nature and a heightened awareness of its delicate balance, feel a deep responsibility to restore harmony and protect the Earth's precious resources. This manifests in various ways – through advocating for sustainable practices, promoting environmental activism, healing damaged ecosystems, and even channeling healing energies into the planet's energetic grid. Their understanding of the interconnectedness of all things extends to the environment, fostering a deep respect for the intricate web of life and a commitment to its preservation.

Starseeds are drawn to Earth by the vision of a future characterized by peace and harmony. Witnessing the suffering caused by conflict, inequality, and injustice, they feel a powerful urge to contribute to a more equitable and compassionate world. They often possess a natural ability to foster understanding, resolve conflict, and promote unity amongst diverse groups. Their unique perspective allows them to transcend limiting beliefs and prejudices, leading them to advocate for peace, social justice, and global cooperation. They may be drawn to careers in humanitarian work, education, or the arts, utilizing their talents to inspire hope and nurture the seeds of a more harmonious future. This vision of a peaceful Earth is not a utopian fantasy, but rather a potential reality that they believe can be achieved through collective effort and conscious evolution.

However, the journey of a Starseed incarnated on Earth is not without its challenges. The dense vibrational frequency of the planet, the pervasive negativity, and the amnesia surrounding their origins can lead to feelings of isolation, confusion, and a sense of not belonging. They may struggle to understand societal norms, feel overwhelmed by the suffering they witness, and grapple with the limitations of the physical body. Yet, these challenges are often seen as necessary trials that serve to strengthen their resolve, refine their abilities, and deepen their empathy for the human experience.

The "Call to Earth" for Starseeds represents a profound commitment to planetary evolution. Driven by a desire to raise consciousness, heal the planet, and lead to an era of peace and harmony, they choose to incarnate on Earth during pivotal times of transformation. Their journey is not always easy, but their unwavering dedication and unique gifts make them invaluable contributors to the collective awakening of humanity. As Earth continues on its path towards a brighter future, the presence of these Starseeds serves as a powerful reminder that we are not alone in this journey, and that the potential for peace, harmony, and enlightenment resides within us all.

IDENTIFYING
Starseed Traits

Having established a foundational understanding of the Starseed concept, we now embark on a journey into the heart of the matter: identifying the unique traits and experiences often associated with those who identify as Starseeds. This exploration is not intended to create rigid categories or definitive labels, but rather to offer a framework for understanding the common threads woven through the narratives of many who resonate with this belief system. It's crucial to remember that these traits are not exclusive to Starseeds, and many non-Starseeds might exhibit some or all of them. However, the convergence of these characteristics is often cited as indicative of a Starseed identity.

One of the most frequently reported traits is a **profound sense of purpose**, often accompanied by a feeling of being "on a mission." This isn't simply an ambition or a career goal; it's a deeply ingrained feeling of having a specific role to play in the world, a contribution that transcends personal gain and aligns with a larger cosmic plan. This sense of purpose can manifest in various ways, from advocating for social justice and environmental protection to pursuing creative endeavors that inspire and uplift others. It's a driving force that often pushes Starseeds beyond their comfort zones, leading them down paths that may seem unconventional or even challenging. This isn't necessarily a conscious choice; it's more of an inner compass, guiding them towards their destined path, often accompanied by a deep-seated feeling of knowing, even without a clear understanding of the "why" or "how." This **internal knowing**, sometimes described as **inner guidance or intuition**, is another hallmark of the Starseed experience.

Heightened intuition and empathy are frequently cited as hallmarks of the Starseed experience. This isn't simply heightened sensitivity; it's an almost preternatural ability to perceive unspoken emotions, energies, and intentions. Starseeds often report feeling deeply connected to the emotions of others, experiencing a level of empathy that can be both a gift and a challenge. This heightened sensitivity can extend beyond human emotions, encompassing a deep connection to the natural world, animals, and even the planet itself. They might find themselves deeply affected by environmental issues, drawn to nature as a source of solace and rejuvenation, and fiercely protective of the planet's well-being. This profound connection to the natural world can manifest in a variety of ways, from an affinity for gardening and outdoor pursuits to a deep commitment to environmental activism. The intensity of their empathy can, at times, feel overwhelming, leading to emotional exhaustion if not managed effectively.

The experience of "otherness" or feeling like an outsider is another common theme among Starseeds. This isn't simply social awkwardness; it's a deeper sense of not quite belonging to the dominant culture or societal norms. Starseeds may feel like they don't fully fit in with their peers or family, experiencing a pervasive sense of not belonging, even amidst supportive relationships. This feeling often stems from a subconscious awareness of their perceived differences and a deeper connection to something beyond the confines of Earthly existence. This sense of "otherness" can be isolating, yet it can also be a source of strength and individuality, pushing them to forge their own paths and embrace their unique perspectives. This feeling of being different can be a catalyst for self-discovery and growth, pushing them to explore their individuality and develop a strong sense of self.

Often intertwined with feelings of otherness is a **recurring sense of displacement or longing for "home."** This isn't necessarily a yearning for a specific physical place but rather a deep-seated longing for something beyond the current reality, a subtle memory of a different existence, a past that feels both familiar and elusive. This longing can manifest as a sense of incompleteness, a feeling that something significant is missing in their lives, despite outward success or fulfilling relationships. This longing is often an underlying current, influencing their choices and experiences, driving them towards a deeper understanding of themselves and their place in the universe. Dreams, vivid imagery, and spontaneous memories may surface, hinting at past lives or experiences that seem to transcend the limitations of human comprehension.

Challenges faced by Starseeds are often rooted in their heightened sensitivity and profound empathy. The intensity of their emotional experience can lead to overwhelm, exhaustion, and even burnout if not properly managed. They may struggle with anxiety, depression, or other mental health challenges as a result of their deep emotional sensitivity. They might find themselves deeply affected by the suffering in the world, leading to feelings of helplessness and despair. Learning to set boundaries, practice self-care, and cultivate healthy coping mechanisms are vital for navigating these challenges. Grounding techniques, meditation, and mindful practices can help to manage overwhelming energies and maintain a sense of balance.

Despite the challenges, the gifts associated with Starseed traits are immense. ***Their heightened intuition and empathy can enable them to connect deeply with others, offer profound compassion, and serve as catalysts for positive change.*** Their sense of purpose can fuel their passion and drive, leading them to achieve remarkable feats and make significant contributions to the world. Their unique perspectives can challenge societal norms, fostering innovation and progress. The journey of a Starseed is a process of embracing their gifts while learning to navigate the challenges, ultimately leading to a greater understanding of themselves, their purpose, and their place within the cosmic design. This integration is a continuous process, requiring self-awareness, self-compassion, and a commitment to personal growth.

Spiritual practices often play a crucial role in the Starseed experience. Meditation, energy work, and other spiritual disciplines can provide tools for managing heightened sensitivity, grounding energy, and accessing inner guidance. Many Starseeds find solace and connection in nature, viewing it as a source of rejuvenation and inspiration. The exploration of past-life memories and connections to other realms can be a powerful aspect of the Starseed journey, offering profound insights and a deeper understanding of their unique path. It's important, however, to approach such explorations with discernment, integrating intuition with critical thinking, and seeking guidance from trusted spiritual mentors or practitioners.

The identification of Starseed traits is a deeply personal journey. ***There's no single test or definitive checklist; it's a process of self-discovery, introspection, and reflection.*** Identifying with the Starseed concept is not about seeking validation or belonging to a specific group; it's about acknowledging the unique aspects of one's experiences and finding a framework that resonates with their inner knowing. The exploration of these characteristics can be a powerful tool for self-understanding and personal growth, leading to greater self-acceptance and a deeper sense of purpose in life.

The potential overlap with other concepts like Indigo Children, Lightworkers, or Empaths is worth acknowledging. Indigo Children are often characterized by heightened intuition, creativity, and empathy, while Lightworkers are dedicated to bringing light and positive energy to the world. Many Starseeds may embody aspects of both, reflecting the fluid and multifaceted nature of these interconnected concepts. Understanding the nuances and overlaps between these concepts can provide a richer, more holistic understanding of individual experiences. Ultimately, the label that resonates most profoundly with an individual is the one that best reflects their unique path and purpose.

The identification of Starseed traits is a complex exploration. The common themes explored here—a deep sense of purpose, heightened intuition and empathy, feelings of otherness, and a profound connection to the cosmos—offer a framework for understanding the experiences of those who identify as Starseeds. However, it's crucial to approach this exploration with an open mind, recognizing the personal and subjective nature of this journey. The journey of a Starseed is one of continuous growth, self-discovery, and integration, ultimately leading to a deeper understanding of one's unique place within the vast cosmic labyrinth.

The challenges and gifts associated with Starseed traits are inextricably linked, requiring a balanced approach of self-awareness, self-compassion, and a commitment to personal growth. By embracing both the light and the shadow, Starseeds can unlock their full potential and contribute their unique gifts to the world.

SHORT LIST:

- **Common Traits and Characteristics:** Recognizing Starseed traits such as:
  - A deep connection to nature and animals
  - A strong sense of empathy and compassion
  - A natural inclination towards healing and helping others
  - A feeling of being different or misunderstood
  - A fascination with space, stars, and extraterrestrial life
  - A strong sense of justice and a desire to fight for the underdog
  - A tendency to feel overwhelmed by negativity and suffering
  - A deep connection to ancient wisdom and esoteric knowledge
  - Experiencing vivid dreams and recurring themes of other worlds

THE ROLE OF
Past Lives

The exploration of past lives holds a significant place within the broader context of the Starseed awakening. For many who identify as Starseeds, the feeling of "otherness," the profound sense of purpose, and the intense empathy they experience are often attributed to memories, not of a previous life on Earth, but of experiences in other realms, on other planets, or within other dimensions. These aren't necessarily literal memories in the conventional sense, but rather intuitive impressions, recurring dreams, or symbolic imagery that hints at a deeper, more expansive reality. These experiences frequently surface during periods of intense spiritual growth or during moments of heightened introspection.

Past life regression therapy, a technique employed by some therapists and spiritual practitioners, can facilitate the uncovering of these potential past-life experiences. This involves guided meditation or hypnotic techniques designed to access the subconscious mind, where memories, beliefs, and experiences –both conscious and unconscious – reside. It's important to note that the validity of past life regression is a subject of ongoing debate, with some within the scientific community expressing skepticism. However, within the context of spiritual exploration and personal growth, the experience can be profoundly transformative, regardless of its literal accuracy. The value lies not necessarily in proving the existence of past lives, but in the insights gained from the process itself.

The experiences uncovered through past life regression can vary widely. Some may recall lives lived on Earth, experiencing different cultures, timelines, and social structures. Others might report experiences that transcend the earthly realm, describing lives spent on other planets, in other dimensions, or as part of a cosmic collective consciousness. These "memories" often reveal details of advanced technologies, unique social structures, or spiritual practices far removed from human experience as we know it. These seemingly fantastical accounts are often intertwined with strong emotions, providing further evidence for their significance in shaping the individual's current identity and experiences.

These unearthed memories, whether related to earthly lives or extraterrestrial encounters, can offer profound insights into the Starseed's present life journey. For example, a recurring theme of service or healing in a past life might explain a current-life passion for social justice or a career in healthcare. A past-life trauma, however obscure, might help illuminate persistent anxieties or fears in the present. The integration of these past-life experiences is therefore essential for personal growth and spiritual development.

The unresolved issues, unresolved emotions, or incomplete tasks from those past lives can manifest as blocks or challenges in the current life, hindering personal growth and fulfillment.`

Exploring past lives isn't solely confined to formal regression sessions. Many Starseeds report spontaneous recall of past life experiences through dreams, vivid imagery, or intuitive flashes.

These memories might be fragmented, symbolic, or intensely emotional. They might be triggered by specific situations, songs, objects, or even scents, prompting a sudden surge of familiarity, recognition, or an inexplicable sense of longing. These spontaneous memories serve as valuable clues, offering glimpses into the individual's spiritual journey and helping to connect the dots between past and present.

The process of integrating past-life experiences is a crucial step in the Starseed awakening. It involves acknowledging and accepting the emotional residue from these past lives, confronting unresolved issues, and ultimately learning from the lessons learned. This might involve seeking professional help from therapists specializing in past-life regression or working with spiritual mentors who guide the process of integration. The goal isn't to dwell on the past but to extract the wisdom and insights that can contribute to a more fulfilling present and future.

Spiritual practices, such as meditation, energy work, and shamanic journeying, can be instrumental in facilitating the process of integrating past life experiences. These practices provide tools for accessing deeper levels of consciousness, accessing subconscious memories, and processing emotional blocks associated with past traumas or unresolved issues. Meditation can create a space for quiet contemplation, allowing these memories to surface gently.

Energy work techniques, like Reiki or energy healing, can help release trapped energies, emotions, and karmic patterns from past lives that continue to impact the present. Shamanic journeying, guided by experienced practitioners, offers a direct path to exploring other realms and connecting with spirit guides who can help navigate these memories and integrate their lessons.

The weight of past lives – a crushing, echoing pressure – bears down on every Starseed's journey. To ignore it is to stumble blindly through a labyrinth of karmic echoes, each twist of the path a phantom limb aching with the memories of forgotten battles.

Understanding these repeating patterns, these soul-deep scars etched across millennia, isn't merely helpful; it's survival. It's the difference between drowning in the ocean of your own otherness and rising, phoenix-like, from the ashes of countless existences. Imagine the scent of burning incense clinging to the air – the aroma of a thousand temples, a thousand deaths, a thousand whispered prayers. Each breath is a taste of eternity, a trace of longing and regret, laced with the iron tang of blood spilled in forgotten wars. Feel the phantom touch of hands across time – the roughness of a medieval craftsman's calluses, the silken caress of a celestial lover, the icy grip of a betrayer in a life long past. This isn't history; **it's you**, meticulously crafted into the very fabric of your being. This variations of lifetimes, once understood, offer not just perspective but an energetic, breathtaking clarity. The sense of purpose isn't a gentle whisper; it's a roaring wind that tears away the illusions of the mundane. Self-compassion becomes less a choice and more a desperate, necessary survival mechanism in the face of such overwhelming experience.

Acceptance? It's a battlefield hard-won, a testament to resilience forged in the fires of a thousand hells. The "otherness," that chilling, isolating feeling of not quite belonging, transforms. It ceases to be a curse and becomes a birthright – a legacy of experiences beyond the grasp of ordinary mortals. Your heightened sensitivity, once a source of pain, is re-evaluated as a gift, a finely-tuned antenna picking up the whispers of the cosmos, the silent screams of a universe begging to be understood. The journey is terrifying, exhilarating, and utterly transformative. Embracing it is not just a choice, it's a declaration of war against the oblivion of forgotten selves.

The merging... it pierces at you. A raw, visceral tearing through the fabric of self, unearthing memories that scream in the silent chambers of your soul. The taste of ash, the phantom touch of ice on skin long gone, the echoing wail of a forgotten grief – these aren't whispers from a distant shore; they're tidal waves crashing over you, threatening to drown you in the ocean of your past lives. This isn't a gentle stroll down memory lane; it's a brutal excavation of the heart. Each fragment of memory, each unearthed trauma, vibrates with a painful intensity that leaves you breathless, gasping for air in a suffocating reality. The weight of centuries bears down, crushing you under the burden of lives lived and lost.

Self-compassion? A fragile raft in a tempestuous sea. Patience? A laughable luxury when your soul is screaming for release. And those trusted mentors, those practitioners you cling to... they are your anchors, yes, but the sea floor feels miles below. Their guidance is a lifeline, yes, but the currents are relentless, and your own strength is tested at every turn. This journey is not your own; it is a symphony of forgotten selves, a chorus of echoing cries demanding to be heard. Each beat is different, each cadence uniquely yours.

There's no roadmap, no promised land. Only the relentless, agonizing, exquisite unfolding of your deepest truth. The pace is dictated not by clocks but by the very rhythm of your soul's rebirth – a fiery phoenix rising from the ashes of countless lifetimes.

The whispers of past lives – unearthed through searing regression, jolting spontaneous recall, or the agonizing ecstasy of spiritual awakening – claw at the edges of the Starseed's identity, a phantom limb twitching with forgotten pain and forgotten glory. But these echoes are merely shards, fragments of a shattered mirror reflecting a truth far greater than its fractured pieces. They offer glimpses into the soul's fantastical odyssey, a kaleidoscope of triumphs and betrayals that resonate with the bone-deep ache of the present. Yet, this life, "this" crucible of flesh and fire, burns with its own incandescent intensity, forging a destiny independent of ancient shadows. The weight of millennia presses down, a suffocating burden of karmic debts and unfulfilled promises. Each past life, a shade of forgotten pain and forgotten aura, a spectral hand reaching across the chasm of time to tug at the present. To succumb to this spectral weight is to be consumed, to become a prisoner of the past. But the Starseed refuses to yield. They feel the sting of old wounds, the chilling echo of past failures, the bitter taste of betrayal on their tongue, the spectral touch of lost loves. Yet, they press onward. The present pulses with a life force both terrifying and exhilarating, a masterpiece of possibilities both glorious and staggering. This is where the true work begins –the brutal, thrilling act of integration. The lessons of ages past must be wrestled into submission, their wisdom forged into a weapon against the insidious whispers of doubt, the gnawing fear of failure. The goal is not mere understanding, but transcendence. It is the forging of a destiny aligned with a purpose so profound it reverberates through eternity, a purpose etched into the very core of their being.

This is a pilgrimage of the soul, a relentless climb up a mountain of self-discovery, each step a victory, each stumble a lesson. It is a life-long crucible, a dance with the divine, a fiery embrace of evolution. The Starseed does not merely awaken to their past; they are **forged anew**, their essence incandescent, their potential limitless, their future an evidence to the unyielding strength of a spirit that has stared into the abyss and emerged triumphant.

The integration of past life experiences, whether through formal regression or through more intuitive means, can significantly enhance the Starseed's understanding of their unique path and purpose. It helps to connect the fragments of a seemingly disparate existence, forging a stronger sense of self and providing a richer, more nuanced perspective on life's complexities. The emotional and spiritual insights gained from this exploration can lead to greater self-acceptance, improved emotional regulation, and a deeper connection with both the inner self and the broader cosmic consciousness. This process is a vital component of the Starseed journey, paving the way for a more conscious, empowered, and purposeful life in the present. By embracing the lessons learned from past lives, Starseeds can unlock their full potential, serve their higher purpose, and contribute their unique gifts to the world. The journey is continuous, a dynamic interplay between past, present, and future, guided by the wisdom gained from a deep understanding of oneself and one's place within the grand cosmic tapestry. It is in this continual evolution that the Starseed truly blossoms, radiating their unique light and contributing their unique gifts to the world.

TRIGGERING THE AWAKENING

The Spark Ignites

The Starseed is believed to carry within them ancient wisdom and a mission to assist in Earth's ascension, is a captivating one. While dormant in most, the potential for awakening lies within, waiting for the right conditions to ignite. This awakening is not a sudden, linear process, but rather a gradual unfolding often triggered by specific life events and guided by the subtle hand of synchronicity. These experiences can act as activation codes, unlocking repressed memories and dormant abilities, propelling the individual towards a deeper understanding of their purpose.

One of the most significant catalysts for Starseed awakening often manifests as intense life experiences. Trauma, loss, and profound moments of connection can serve as the "activation codes" that jolt the soul from its earthly slumber. Trauma, though devastating, can shatter the illusion of the mundane, forcing a confrontation with deeper realities. It can strip away superficial identities and expose the raw, unadulterated core, the very essence of the Starseed soul. Similarly, the loss of a loved one, particularly a soul connection, can trigger a profound sense of longing and a yearning for understanding that transcends the limitations of physical existence. This yearning can lead to exploration of spiritual realms and a search for the answer to the fundamental question: "What is the meaning of life, and what is my role in it?"

Conversely, moments of profound connection, particularly with nature, animals, or like-minded souls, can also act as powerful triggers. These experiences resonate with a deeper part of the self, a forgotten homeland echoing within the soul. They can awaken latent abilities, such as heightened empathy, intuition, or even a connection to universal energies. These connections remind the Starseed of their inherent interconnectedness and their innate ability to tap into a larger field of consciousness. Such moments can ignite a spark of recognition, a feeling of "coming home," even if the home is not found on this planet.

While life events act as the initial spark, the journey is sustained and guided by the power of synchronicity. These "meaningful coincidences" are more than just random occurrences; they are subtle nudges from the universe, confirmations that the individual is on the right path. Seeing specific numbers repeatedly, encountering relevant information at precisely the right time, or meeting individuals who hold keys to understanding are all examples of these synchronicities. They are breadcrumbs on the path, leading the awakening Starseed towards self-discovery and the fulfillment of their mission.

Recognizing the significance of synchronicity is crucial. It requires a shift in perspective, a willingness to see beyond the mundane and embrace the interconnectedness of all things. Paying attention to these signs and interpreting their meaning requires intuition and a deep trust in the universe. For example, a Starseed might repeatedly encounter information about a specific star system or civilization. This synchronistic occurrence could be a sign that they have a past life connection to that place or that they are meant to learn from its wisdom. By acknowledging these signs and actively seeking understanding, the Starseed can gain valuable insights into their purpose and navigate their awakening journey with greater clarity.

The awakening of a Starseed is a profound and transformative process, triggered by significant life events and guided by the subtle hand of synchronicity. We must understand that trauma, loss, and moments of profound connection can act as activation codes, unlocking repressed memories and dormant abilities. Recognizing and interpreting the significance of synchronicities provides ongoing guidance and reassurance that the individual is on the right path. By embracing these experiences and trusting in the wisdom of the universe, the Starseed can step into their true potential and contribute to the ascension of Earth, fulfilling the ancient contract they made before incarnating on this planet. The spark ignites, illuminating the path towards a brighter future, not just for the individual, but for all of humanity.

The Significance of Dreams and Intuition

The journey of a Starseed is often marked not only by memories of past lives, but also by an acutely heightened intuition and a vibrant dreamscape. These experiences are not mere coincidences; they are integral components of the awakening process, offering invaluable guidance and insights into the Starseed's unique purpose and path.

While the exploration of past lives provides a foundation for understanding the karmic imprints and soul lessons that shape the present, the realm of dreams and intuition offers a direct line of communication to the inner wisdom, a connection to the higher self, and sometimes, even glimpses into future possibilities.

Recurring dreams, for many Starseeds, are far from random. They often contain potent symbolism, rich imagery, and narratives that echo themes present in their waking lives, or reveal patterns from past lives. These dreams may involve celestial bodies, unfamiliar landscapes, advanced technologies, or encounters with beings that seem beyond human comprehension. These aren't simply night-time fantasies; they are often messages from the subconscious, attempts by the soul to communicate profound truths and guide the individual toward their higher purpose. The imagery within these dreams often acts as a symbolic language, requiring careful attention and interpretation. A recurring image of flight, for instance, might symbolize spiritual ascension or freedom from limitations. A recurring motif of water could represent the flow of emotions or the subconscious mind. The key lies not in seeking literal interpretations but in understanding the symbolic meaning within the context of the individual's life and experiences.

Journaling dreams, paying attention to recurring symbols, and considering the emotional context of the dream narrative are essential steps in this process. Working with a dream interpreter or therapist experienced in symbolic analysis can also prove incredibly beneficial.

Beyond recurring dreams, many Starseeds report experiencing vivid, highly symbolic dreams that seem to transcend the ordinary. These dreams might contain precognitive elements, offering glimpses into future events or potential outcomes. Such experiences, while initially disorienting, can serve as powerful tools for navigating life's challenges. They can highlight potential pitfalls, signal impending opportunities, or even offer guidance on how to best approach difficult situations. These precognitive dreams, however, should not be interpreted as fixed destinies. They are instead potential pathways, offering a range of possibilities and allowing for conscious choice and intervention. The ability to discern precognitive dreams from ordinary dreams often requires developing a heightened sense of self-awareness and paying close attention to the emotional tone and the level of detail within the dream narrative.

Intuition, a powerful ally on the Starseed journey, is another crucial aspect of this awakening. It's the inner voice, a subtle yet persistent guiding force, that often whispers (or sometimes shouts!) the right path to follow. For Starseeds, intuition is frequently amplified, acting as a compass guiding them toward their life's purpose and helping them navigate the complexities of their journey. This intuition may manifest as a gut feeling, a sudden insight, or a clear knowing that transcends logical reasoning. It might appear as a strong sense of knowing what to say, where to go, or whom to trust, often in situations where rational analysis would provide little guidance.

The development and refinement of intuition is a crucial aspect of the Starseed awakening. Several techniques can facilitate this process. Mindfulness practices, such as meditation and deep breathing exercises, quiet the mental chatter, creating space for the subtle voice of intuition to be heard. Spending time in nature, immersing oneself in the beauty and tranquility of the natural world, can also help to connect with the intuitive flow. Energy work, including practices like Reiki or qigong, can help clear energetic blockages that may be hindering intuitive awareness. Journaling, particularly focused free-writing, can also be invaluable, providing a space to explore thoughts, feelings, and intuitions without judgment.

The intuitive guidance received shouldn't be dismissed as mere coincidence or fanciful thinking. It's essential to approach this inner wisdom with respect and attentiveness, learning to differentiate between intuition and fear-based thinking or ego-driven impulses. The integration of intuition into daily decision-making is a gradual process. Start with small decisions – choosing a restaurant, selecting a route – and gradually expand to larger choices as you gain confidence in your intuitive abilities. It's important to remember that intuition doesn't always present itself as a clear-cut answer. It can be subtle, manifesting as a feeling, an impression, or a subtle shift in energy. Learning to trust this inner guidance and act upon it will not only improve your decision-making but also contribute to a greater sense of alignment and purpose.

The significance of dreams and intuition extends beyond personal decision-making. They play a crucial role in the spiritual growth of a Starseed. These experiences offer a pathway to connect with higher consciousness, accessing wisdom and guidance that transcends the limitations of the physical world. Dreams can provide symbolic representations of spiritual lessons, revealing hidden patterns and unresolved issues that need attention. Intuition acts as a compass, guiding you towards experiences and relationships that contribute to your spiritual evolution. Through dreams and intuition, Starseeds can gain insights into their karmic patterns, uncover hidden talents, and access a deeper understanding of their unique place within the cosmos.

Developing a strong connection to one's inner wisdom is a lifelong journey that unfolds organically as one grows spiritually. It's essential to nurture these abilities, treating dreams and intuition as valuable sources of guidance and self-discovery, rather than dismissing them as whimsical imaginings. Consistent practice and conscious awareness will enhance the ability to decipher their messages and integrate their wisdom into daily life. ***The power of dreams and intuition is not a mere addition to the Starseed experience; it is integral to the awakening process, offering a powerful connection to the higher self, a deeper understanding of purpose, and a guide towards fulfilling one's true potential within the grand cosmic design.*** It is through this harmonious blend of past-life understanding, heightened intuition, and vivid dream landscapes that the Starseed truly blossoms, realizing their unique gifts and contributions to the world. The journey itself is a piece of evidence to the power of inner wisdom, a continuous unfolding of the soul's inherent potential. The ability to listen to this inner voice and translate the messages conveyed through dreams and intuition is a cornerstone of the Starseed awakening, leading to greater self-awareness, a profound sense of purpose, and a life aligned with one's higher calling. This intimate connection with the inner self provides not only personal growth and fulfillment, but also the capacity to contribute uniquely to the collective consciousness and the unfolding evolution of the universe. The process of integrating this inner wisdom is a continuous evolution, requiring patience, self-compassion, and consistent dedication to personal growth. It is a transformative journey, leading towards a more fulfilling life, a deeper connection to the cosmos, and a significant contribution to the greater whole. The integration of this knowledge is an ongoing process, a lifelong endeavor of self-discovery, where the Starseed steadily uncovers their true potential and purpose, revealing the magnificent tapestry of their existence within the universe.

DECODING THE SELF

Dreams, Energies, *and the* Awakening Journey

The human experience is an incredible design created between the conscious and unconscious, the physical and the metaphysical. As we embark on the journey of self-discovery, we often encounter whispers from realms beyond our immediate perception. Dreams, energy sensitivities, and physical manifestations can act as signposts, guiding us towards a deeper understanding of our past lives, our mission on Earth, and our connection to the cosmos. These phenomena, often dismissed by the dominant materialistic paradigm, offer profound insights into the awakening process, revealing the intricate layers of our being.

Dreams, in particular, serve as a portal to the symbolic language of the unconscious. Often bizarre and seemingly nonsensical, they are not merely random firings of neurons but rather a carefully crafted narrative encoded with personal and archetypal symbols. Decoding this language allows us to access the hidden depths of our psyche, unlocking clues about unresolved traumas from past lives, forgotten skills, and the overarching purpose we are meant to fulfill in this incarnation. Carl Jung, a pioneer in dream analysis, believed that dreams are a form of compensation, highlighting aspects of ourselves that we neglect in our waking lives. Recurring dreams, for example, often point to unresolved issues that demand our attention and integration. Animals, environments, and even everyday objects in our dreams can hold symbolic weight, representing aspects of our personality, relationships, and the direction of our life path. By meticulously recording and analyzing our dreams, and by learning the language of symbolism, we can begin to piece together the fragmented memories of our past lives, gaining awareness of karmic patterns and the lessons we are here to learn. This understanding, in turn, empowers us to make conscious choices that align with our soul's purpose and break free from limiting cycles.

Furthermore, an integral part of the awakening process involves heightened energy sensitivities and accompanying physical manifestations. As our consciousness expands, we become increasingly attuned to the subtle energies that permeate our environment and our own bodies. This increased sensitivity can manifest as an awareness of energy fields surrounding people and objects, an enhanced intuition, and a profound connection to nature. However, this heightened awareness can also bring challenges. We may become more susceptible to the emotional states of others, experiencing empathy to an overwhelming degree. Environmental factors like electromagnetic fields (EMFs) or synthetic materials can trigger physical discomfort, leading to fatigue, headaches, or digestive issues. Changes in sleep patterns are also common, with individuals experiencing insomnia, vivid dreams, or even astral projections. These physical manifestations, often unexplained by conventional medicine, are not necessarily signs of illness but rather indications of the body's adaptation to higher frequencies of energy.

Understanding the connection between these energy sensitivities and the physical body is crucial for navigating the awakening process with grace and ease. ***The body serves as a conduit for energy, and when it is overloaded or blocked, it can manifest as physical discomfort.*** Learning grounding techniques, such as spending time in nature, practicing meditation, or engaging in physical activities, can help to regulate energy flow and alleviate these symptoms. Furthermore, paying attention to our diet and lifestyle choices is essential. Processed foods, excessive caffeine, and prolonged exposure to technology can all disrupt our energy field and exacerbate physical sensitivities. By cultivating a holistic approach to well-being, encompassing physical, emotional, and spiritual needs, we can create a supportive environment for the awakening process to unfold naturally.

The exploration of dreams, energy sensitivities, and physical manifestations is a deeply personal and transformative journey. It requires a willingness to embrace the unknown, to trust our intuition, and to listen to the subtle whispers of our inner guidance. By decoding the symbolic language of dreams, we can unlock the secrets of our past lives and gain clarity on our present mission. By understanding and managing our energy sensitivities, we can navigate the physical challenges of the awakening process and connect more deeply with the cosmos. As we embark on this path of self-discovery, we begin to realize that we are not merely individual beings but integral parts of a vast and interconnected universe, each playing a unique and vital role in the grand cosmic dance.

NAVIGATING THE AWAKENING PROCESS

Overcoming *the* Challenges *of the* Dark Night *of the* Soul

The awakening process, a profound shift in consciousness characterized by increased self-awareness, a questioning of societal norms, and a desire for deeper meaning, is often depicted as a radiant journey towards enlightenment. However, this journey is rarely a linear ascent into blissful understanding. Instead, it often involves navigating turbulent waters and confronting the shadows within. One of the most challenging aspects of this transformation is the "Dark Night of the Soul," a period marked by intense feelings of isolation, doubt, fear, and a seeming loss of connection to the world, requiring specific tools and strategies to overcome.

The Dark Night of the Soul is not merely a period of sadness or depression; it's a profound dismantling of the ego and its illusions. It is a necessary stage where old beliefs, outdated identities, and ingrained patterns of thinking are challenged and often crumble under the weight of newly acquired awareness. This can feel like a personal apocalypse, a complete loss of bearings, and a terrifying uncertainty about the future. The familiar structures that once provided comfort and security dissolve, leaving one feeling vulnerable and lost in a vast, unfamiliar landscape.

Feelings of isolation are a common companion during this phase. As one's perspective shifts, the individual may find themselves feeling increasingly detached from friends, family, and even society as a whole. Conversations that once felt meaningful can now seem superficial or even triggering. This disengagement can lead to feelings of loneliness and alienation, amplifying the sense of being alone in a world that no longer resonates.

The Dark Night often unearths deep-seated doubts and fears. The questioning of long-held beliefs can trigger existential anxieties, leading one to question the very foundation of their reality. Fears surrounding mortality, purpose, and the unknown can surface, creating a sense of unease and insecurity. This process can be particularly challenging as it often requires acknowledging and confronting aspects of oneself that were previously hidden or repressed.

Navigating this challenging terrain requires a combination of self-compassion, mindful awareness, and a commitment to inner work. Acknowledging and validating the feelings that arise is crucial. Suppressing or denying these emotions only prolongs the suffering. Instead, allow yourself to feel the pain, the fear, and the doubt without judgment. Recognize that these feelings are temporary and part of a natural process of transformation.

Mindfulness practices, such as meditation and conscious breathing, can offer powerful tools for navigating difficult emotions. By observing thoughts and feelings without getting caught up in them, one can develop a sense of detachment and create space for greater clarity and understanding. Meditation can also help to cultivate a sense of inner calm and stability, providing a much-needed anchor amidst the storm.

Seeking support from trusted sources is also essential. This could involve connecting with a therapist, spiritual advisor, or support group where one can share their experiences and receive guidance. Talking to others who have navigated similar challenges can provide validation, reassurance, and practical advice. Remember that you are not alone in this journey, and connection with others can significantly ease the burden.

The Dark Night of the Soul often necessitates a period of introspection and self-reflection. This is a time to re-evaluate values, beliefs, and priorities. By honestly examining one's life and identifying areas that are no longer aligned with their authentic self, one can begin to rebuild a more meaningful and fulfilling existence. This process may involve letting go of old patterns, shedding limiting beliefs, and embracing new perspectives.

Navigating the awakening process, particularly the Dark Night of the Soul, is a challenging but ultimately transformative experience. By acknowledging the difficult emotions that arise, practicing mindfulness, seeking support, and engaging in self-reflection, one can navigate the depths of darkness and emerge with greater wisdom, resilience, and a deeper connection to oneself and the world. The Dark Night, while painful, is not an end but a necessary passage towards a more authentic and fulfilling life. It is a testament to the courage and strength of the human spirit to continuously evolve and seek deeper truth.

Overcoming Challenges *and* Embracing Your Gift

The journey of a Starseed, as we've explored, is often one of profound awakening, marked by vivid dreams, heightened intuition, and a deep sense of connection to something larger than oneself. Yet, this unique path is not without its challenges. Many Starseeds find themselves grappling with feelings of isolation, a sense of not quite belonging within the conventional structures of society. This feeling of otherness, while sometimes unsettling, is often a key indicator of the Starseed's distinct energy and purpose. It's a recognition of their unique vibrational frequency, a frequency that resonates with a different rhythm than the dominant societal melody.

This disconnect can manifest in various ways. Many Starseeds report feeling profoundly misunderstood, their heightened sensitivity leading to emotional overwhelm in environments that lack empathy or understanding. Simple everyday interactions, which might pass unnoticed by others, can trigger intense emotional responses in a Starseed. The noise of a crowded room, the harshness of certain words, the unspoken tensions within a group—all these can be amplified and interpreted with a depth of feeling that leaves the Starseed feeling drained, overwhelmed, or even physically ill. This intense sensitivity is not a weakness; it is a gift, an enhanced capacity for empathy and connection, a finely tuned antenna picking up the subtle vibrations of the world around them.

This heightened sensitivity, however, can lead to feelings of isolation. The Starseed may find themselves struggling to connect with others on a deeper level, feeling like an outsider looking in, longing for a connection that mirrors their own depth of feeling.

The conventional societal structures, often geared towards conformity and a suppression of intense emotion, can feel suffocating and restrictive.

The Starseed's yearning for authenticity and deeper meaning may clash with societal expectations of conformity and superficiality. This dissonance can lead to feelings of frustration, disillusionment, and a sense of being out of place.

Overcoming these challenges requires a shift in perspective. The feeling of isolation, for instance, is not an indication of failure or inadequacy, but rather an invitation to cultivate self-acceptance and embrace one's unique path. Instead of striving to fit into pre-existing molds, the Starseed needs to create their own space, a sanctuary where their heightened sensitivity is not a liability but a strength. This may involve setting boundaries, carefully choosing the environments and relationships that nurture their soul, and learning to detach from the expectations of those who don't understand their unique perspective.

Building supportive relationships is crucial for navigating these challenges. Finding others who resonate with the Starseed's energy, who understand their sensitivity and appreciate their unique perspective, can provide invaluable support and validation. This may involve seeking out like-minded individuals through online communities, workshops, or spiritual groups. The shared experiences and understanding fostered within these communities can create a powerful sense of belonging and help alleviate feelings of isolation. It's important to remember that connection doesn't always mean large groups; sometimes, one deep and meaningful relationship can provide more support than many superficial ones.

Finding your unique path requires introspection and self-discovery.

The challenges Starseeds face often serve as catalysts for personal growth. By exploring these experiences, understanding the root causes of their sensitivity, and embracing their gifts, they can transform adversity into opportunity. Journaling, meditation, and mindfulness practices can be invaluable tools in this process. These practices provide space for self-reflection, allowing the Starseed to process their emotions, understand their reactions, and cultivate a greater sense of self-awareness.

Self-compassion is essential in navigating these challenges. The Starseed journey is not a race; it's a lifelong process of growth and evolution. There will be times of frustration, moments of doubt, and periods where the path seems unclear. During these times, it is crucial to extend the same kindness and understanding to oneself as one would offer a dear friend. Self-criticism and self-judgment will only exacerbate the challenges, hindering the process of self-discovery. Instead, focus on self-acceptance, celebrating your strengths, acknowledging your vulnerabilities, and embracing the journey with compassion and grace.

Managing emotional sensitivity requires conscious effort.

Developing healthy coping mechanisms is paramount. This may involve setting boundaries, learning to say no, and prioritizing self-care. Practicing grounding techniques, such as spending time in nature, engaging in physical activity, or listening to calming music, can help regulate emotional intensity. Exploring therapeutic approaches, such as energy healing or somatic experiencing, can provide additional support in managing emotional overwhelm. The key is to find what works best for you and to utilize those techniques consistently, creating a personalized toolkit for navigating moments of emotional intensity.

Understanding the root causes of the challenges is vital. ***Many Starseeds carry karmic imprints from past lives or ancestral lineages that contribute to their sensitivity.*** Exploring these patterns through past-life regression, ancestral healing, or other spiritual practices can offer invaluable insights and facilitate healing. This is not about dwelling on the past, but about understanding the present, acknowledging the influence of past experiences, and using that understanding to create a more empowered future. This integration of past experiences into the present moment allows for the release of trapped energies and the emergence of a more whole and balanced self.

**Embracing your unique gifts is vital.
The heightened sensitivity, the deep empathy, the intuitive abilities—these are not flaws, but extraordinary strengths.
Finding ways to express these gifts, whether through creative pursuits, spiritual service, or interpersonal connection, can bring profound fulfillment and a sense of purpose.**

This may involve channeling your energy into activities that resonate with your soul, aligning your actions with your values, and contributing your unique talents to the world. The process of self-discovery unfolds as you actively engage with the world, using your innate gifts to make a positive impact.

Finding your path is an unfolding journey, it's a process of continuous learning, growth, and self-discovery. There will be moments of uncertainty, challenges that test your resilience, and detours that lead to unexpected opportunities. Embrace these experiences as part of your unique journey, trusting that you are exactly where you are meant to be, and that your path is unfolding perfectly, even amidst apparent adversity. This trust in the process is essential, fostering a sense of peace and allowing for a deeper connection to your inner wisdom.

The journey of a Starseed is not one of conformity, but of self-discovery. It's about embracing your unique gifts, navigating your challenges with self-compassion, and finding your unique path in the world. By understanding and accepting the aspects of your journey, you not only overcome the challenges but also fully embody your gifts, contributing your unique essence to the unfolding tapestry of life. It's a journey of transformation, a process of awakening to your true potential, and a path towards a life of profound purpose and fulfillment.

This self-discovery is an active engagement with yourself, your sensitivities, your gifts, and your connection to the universe, a continuous dance between challenge and grace, leading to a deeper understanding of self and a more meaningful contribution to the world.

It is this commitment to the process that allows the Starseed to truly shine, radiating their unique light and contributing to the evolution of consciousness itself. The ongoing exploration of your inner landscape, the dedication to self-compassion, and the unwavering commitment to your own unique path are the key elements that empower the Starseed to not only overcome challenges but to transform them into opportunities for profound growth and meaningful contribution to the world.

UNDERSTANDING
Universal Energy

Understanding the concept of universal energy is a crucial step to recognizing the Starseed experience. It's the underlying current that connects every aspect of our being, from the subatomic particles within our cells to the vast expanse of the cosmos. Many spiritual traditions have described this energy using different names– **Chi, Prana, Ki,** or simply**, Life Force**. Modern physics, too, hints at a unifying field, a fundamental energy that underlies the apparent diversity of the universe. This universal energy isn't a mere abstract concept; it's a tangible force, a vibrant, pulsating field of consciousness that permeates all existence.

One way to comprehend this energy is through the lens of interconnectedness. Every particle, every atom, every being in the universe is fundamentally connected. This connection isn't simply metaphorical; it's a direct, energetic linkage. Think of the universe as a vast ocean, and each of us as individual waves. While we may appear distinct, we are all part of the same ocean, inseparable from the whole. The actions of one wave impact others, creating ripples that spread throughout the entire ocean. Similarly, our thoughts, emotions, and actions have a ripple effect, influencing the entire energetic field of the universe.

This interconnectedness is crucial to understanding the power of intention. When we direct our attention and focus our energy on a particular goal, we are actively influencing the universal energy field. The universe, in its infinite wisdom, responds to our intentions. This isn't about manipulating the universe to bend to our will; it's about aligning ourselves with the inherent flow of energy, allowing the universe to guide us towards our highest potential. The more focused and aligned our intentions are, the more potent their effect on the universal energy field.

Understanding the flow of energy within our own bodies is also essential. The human body is not just a physical vessel; it's a complex energetic system, a microcosm of the universe itself. Energy flows through our bodies through various pathways, known as meridians in traditional Chinese medicine. These meridians are not visible to the naked eye, but their existence is felt through the sensations of energy flow. When this energy flow is blocked or disrupted, it can manifest as physical or emotional imbalances. Techniques like acupuncture and energy healing work by clearing these blockages and restoring the natural flow of energy.

The Starseed's heightened sensitivity often allows them to perceive this energetic flow more acutely. They may experience this as an intuitive understanding of energy dynamics, a heightened sense of empathy, or an extraordinary ability to feel the emotions and intentions of others. ***This sensitivity is not simply a gift; it's a responsibility.*** It's a call to cultivate a deeper understanding of universal energy and to harness its power for personal growth and spiritual transformation.

Various modalities can help access and utilize universal energy.

MEDITATION is a powerful tool for connecting with this energy, allowing us to quiet the mental chatter and tune into the subtle vibrations of the universe. Through meditation, we can cultivate a deeper sense of inner peace, expand our consciousness, and connect to a higher source of energy. Yoga and Tai Chi are further examples of practices that align us with the flow of universal energy, enhancing our physical, emotional, and spiritual well-being. These are not merely physical exercises; they are energetic practices that cultivate balance, strength, and connection with the universal flow.

ENERGY HEALING modalities, such as Reiki and Pranic Healing, work directly with the body's energy field to clear blockages, restore balance, and promote healing. These modalities harness the universal life force energy to facilitate the natural healing process of the body. The practitioner acts as a conduit for this energy, channeling it to the recipient to promote physical, emotional, and spiritual well-being.

NATURE provides a powerful source of universal energy. Spending time outdoors, connecting with the earth, can significantly enhance our energetic well-being. Walking barefoot on the grass, swimming in the ocean, or simply sitting under a tree – these simple acts can reconnect us to the natural energy of the earth, grounding us and restoring our balance. The earth itself is a powerful source of energy, constantly radiating life-giving energy, replenishing and nourishing all life forms.

WORKING WITH CRYSTALS can also enhance our connection to universal energy. Different crystals possess unique vibrational frequencies that can enhance our energy field and promote balance and healing.

By holding a crystal or placing it on the body, we can tap into its unique energy signature, helping us to clear blockages, energize our bodies, and promote emotional and spiritual growth. Crystals act as energetic amplifiers, enhancing our connection to the universal energy field.

SOUND THERAPY is another effective method for accessing and utilizing universal energy. Different sounds and frequencies can influence our energy field, creating a feeling of deep relaxation and inner peace. Sound baths, specifically, utilize various instruments to create a healing environment, allowing the individual to connect with the universal energy through the vibrational frequencies of the sounds. Sound acts as a bridge, connecting us to the energy field and facilitating harmony and balance.

VISUALIZATION can also be profoundly helpful. By vividly imagining ourselves connected to a source of universal energy, we can actively draw that energy into our bodies, enhancing our vitality, strength, and overall well-being.

Visualization is a powerful tool to create and manifest our intentions, amplifying the effects of our conscious effort.

However, it's crucial to approach the harnessing of universal energy with intentionality and respect. It's not about seeking power or control; it's about aligning ourselves with the natural flow of energy, honoring its wisdom and allowing it to guide us. This requires a conscious intention to use this energy for good, for healing, for personal growth, and for the benefit of others.

Approaching the practice with humility and respect ensures responsible and ethical engagement with the vast potential of universal energy.

This understanding of universal energy goes beyond mere intellectual knowledge; it's an experiential journey. It's a process of self-discovery, of tuning into the subtle vibrations of the universe, and of aligning ourselves with the natural flow of energy. The Starseed's heightened sensitivity is a powerful asset in this journey, allowing them to perceive and interact with universal energy in ways others might not. This sensitivity can be nurtured and developed, providing a deeper connection to the cosmic scheme and a more profound understanding of one's place within the grand tapestry of existence.

The challenges faced by Starseeds often serve as catalysts for this energetic growth, pushing them towards a deeper understanding and connection with the universal energy field.

This deeper connection unlocks their inherent abilities and enhances their capacity for self-healing, personal growth, and fulfilling their unique purpose on this planet. Through consistent practice and conscious intention, Starseeds can harness the power of universal energy to navigate the complexities of life with grace, resilience, and a profound sense of purpose. The journey is one of continuous unfolding, a dynamic interplay between the inner world and the vast cosmos, a process of becoming fully embodied and deeply connected to the living energy that sustains all life.

EMBRACING YOUR COSMIC HERITAGE

Unveiling Your Purpose Through Remembering Star Origins

The whisper of the cosmos echoes within us all, a silent resonance of star dust and ancient memories. For those who feel a profound sense of disconnect from the everyday, a longing for something more, the answer may lie in embracing their cosmic heritage. As we analyzed so far, the concept of "Starseeds," souls who originated from other star systems and incarnated on Earth to assist in its evolution, offers a compelling framework for understanding this feeling and unlocking a deeper sense of purpose. By remembering our possible star origins, we can tap into the wisdom and skills honed across millennia and contribute to the transformation of our planet.

The idea of Starseeds rests on the belief that Earth is not isolated, but connected to a vast framework of interstellar civilizations. Different star systems, each with its unique energy signature and developmental trajectory, have seeded humanity with their unique attributes. Exploring these potential origins opens a doorway to self-discovery and understanding the specific gifts we bring to the table. While not everyone resonates with this concept, and skepticism is healthy, exploring these ideas can be a powerful tool for personal growth and finding meaning.

One of the most commonly mentioned Starseed origins is the **Pleiades**. Inhabitants of this cluster, located in the constellation Taurus, are often described as possessing a loving and nurturing energy. **Pleiadian Starseeds** are drawn to healing arts, environmentalism, and creating harmonious relationships. They are often empathic and sensitive, feeling deeply for the suffering of others. Their purpose often revolves around fostering compassion, promoting unity, and radiating unconditional love into the world. The inherent desire to create safe and supportive environments can be a telltale sign of a Pleiadian connection.

Another significant origin is **Sirius**. Known for their highly evolved beings with advanced technology and spiritual wisdom, Sirians are pioneers and innovators. **Sirian Starseeds** often possess a keen intellect, a thirst for knowledge, and a natural aptitude for science, technology, and metaphysics. They strive for progress and often feel driven to find innovative solutions to complex problems. Their purpose might involve bridging the gap between science and spirituality, accelerating technological advancements that benefit humanity, and sharing their profound understanding of the universe.

In contrast to the technological focus of Sirius, the **Arcturians** are often revered as masters of healing and emotional balance. Originating from Arcturus, the brightest star in the constellation Boötes, these beings possess a deep understanding of energy and its influence on the human body and mind. **Arcturian Starseeds** are drawn to holistic health practices, energy healing modalities, and promoting emotional well-being. Their purpose often involves helping others heal from trauma, achieve emotional equilibrium, and raise the vibrational frequency of the planet through love and compassion.

The **Lyran** system holds a special place in the Starseed narrative as it is often considered the ancestral home of many humanoid races. **Lyran Starseeds** carry within them ancient memories of a time before the galactic wars, a time of unity and harmony. They are often drawn to leadership roles, community building, and restoring balance to broken systems. Their purpose may involve advocating for justice, creating sustainable communities, and promoting peace and reconciliation.

Finally, the inhabitants of **Andromeda** are known for their focus on creating harmonious societies. **Andromedan Starseeds** are often drawn to social justice, environmental activism, and community organizing. They possess a natural talent for diplomacy and negotiation and strive to create systems that are fair and equitable for all. Their purpose often involves inspiring social change, promoting sustainable practices, and fostering a sense of unity and interconnectedness among all beings.

Ultimately, embracing your cosmic heritage is a deeply personal journey. It requires introspection, self-reflection, and a willingness to explore the possibilities beyond the confines of conventional thinking. While the identification of a specific star origin can provide validation and a sense of belonging, it is crucial to remember that these are merely frameworks for understanding ourselves and our purpose on Earth. The specific skills and talents we bring to the planet are unique and multifaceted, shaped by our experiences and our individual soul contracts.

By exploring different Starseed origins, we can gain a deeper understanding of our innate abilities, our passions, and our potential to contribute to the evolution of humanity. Whether we resonate with the nurturing energy of the Pleiades, the innovative spirit of Sirius, the healing wisdom of Arcturus, the ancestral connection of Lyra, or the harmonious vision of Andromeda, embracing our cosmic heritage can unlock a profound sense of purpose and empower us to create a better future for ourselves and for the planet. The stars call to us, reminding us of our ancient origins and inviting us to embrace our unique role in the grand cosmic drama unfolding on Earth. The time to listen is now.

HARNESSING YOUR
Personal Energy Field

We've explored the vast ocean of universal energy, its interconnectedness, and its responsiveness to our intentions. Now, let's dive deeper into the personal aspect of this energetic landscape– your own personal energy field. Think of it as your individual wave within that vast ocean, unique yet intrinsically connected to the whole. This energy field, often referred to as the aura, is a dynamic and vibrant expression of your being, a luminous sheath of energy that surrounds and permeates your physical body. It's a reflection of your physical, emotional, mental, and spiritual state. A healthy, vibrant aura radiates strength, vitality, and a sense of well-being, while a depleted or unbalanced aura can manifest as physical or emotional discomfort, fatigue, and susceptibility to illness.

Understanding your personal energy field is crucial for harnessing the power of universal energy. Just as a skilled surfer learns to ride the waves, you can learn to navigate and utilize the currents of your own energy field. This involves becoming acutely aware of its fluctuations, identifying blockages, and developing techniques to clear, balance, and strengthen it. Think of your aura as a finely tuned instrument; when it's in harmony, it resonates with clarity and strength, allowing you to connect more easily with the universal energy field. When it's out of tune, it dampens your connection, making it harder to access your inner wisdom and your highest potential.

One of the most significant factors influencing your energy field is your emotional state. Negative emotions like anger, fear, and resentment tend to contract and constrict the energy flow, creating blockages and imbalances. Conversely, positive emotions like joy, love, and gratitude expand and harmonize the energy field, promoting a sense of well-being and vitality. Imagine your emotions as colors painting your aura. Fear might cast a grey shadow, while love illuminates it with a radiant golden light. By cultivating positive emotions, you are essentially painting your aura with vibrant, life-affirming hues, strengthening its resilience and radiance. This conscious cultivation of positive emotional states is a powerful tool for managing and enhancing your personal energy field.

Various practices can assist in clearing and balancing your energy field. Grounding techniques, such as walking barefoot on the earth, spending time in nature, or simply sitting quietly and focusing on your breath, can help to connect you to the earth's stabilizing energy, drawing negative energy away from your aura and replenishing it with grounding earth energy. Visualization is another powerful tool. Imagine a golden white light emanating from the earth, entering your body through your feet, washing away any stagnant or negative energy, and filling your aura with vibrant, life-giving energy. This simple practice, done regularly, can significantly enhance your energetic well-being.

Meditation is a profound practice for connecting with and managing your energy field. Regular meditation helps to calm the mind, reduce stress, and promote a state of inner peace. As your mind quiets, you become more attuned to the subtle energies within and around you, gaining a clearer sense of your aura's state. Guided meditations, specifically designed for energy clearing and balancing, can help to identify and address any energetic blockages, restoring the natural flow of energy within your aura. The enhanced awareness gained through meditation is crucial for self-regulation and maintaining an energetic equilibrium.

Energy healing modalities, like Reiki and Pranic Healing, can provide further support in clearing and balancing your energy field. These practices involve the practitioner channeling universal energy to clear blockages, restore balance, and promote healing. While you can practice many aspects of energy management independently, energy healing sessions can be valuable for deeper energetic work and overcoming more persistent imbalances. These modalities offer a potent opportunity to address any energetic blockages or imbalances that may be hindering your connection with your own personal energy field and the universal energy field.

The use of crystals can also be beneficial in enhancing your energy field. Different crystals possess unique vibrational frequencies that can resonate with and enhance specific aspects of your energy. Amethyst is known for its calming and purifying properties, helping to clear negative energy from your aura. Rose quartz is associated with love and compassion, promoting emotional healing and enhancing your ability to receive and give love. By carefully selecting crystals that resonate with your intention, you can enhance your energetic well-being and promote healing and balance in your energy field. Experiment with different crystals, allowing yourself to intuitively select the ones that call to you. The connection is not just a belief, but a subtle vibrational resonance.

Sound therapy also offers a powerful means of working with your energy field. Different sounds and frequencies can influence the energy flow within your aura, creating a feeling of deep relaxation and harmony. Sound baths, in particular, utilize various instruments to create a healing environment, allowing you to connect with your energy field through the vibrational frequencies of the sounds. The resonance of sound acts as a catalyst, gently harmonizing the energetic vibrations within and around you.

Strengthening your personal energy field is an ongoing process, not a one-time event. It requires consistent practice, self-awareness, and a commitment to self-care. Just as physical fitness requires regular exercise, energetic fitness requires regular energetic practices. Incorporate these practices into your daily routine, making them a natural part of your self-care regimen. Consider keeping a journal to track your progress, noting any shifts in your emotional state, energy levels, and overall well-being.

Beyond the practical techniques, it's essential to cultivate an inner attitude that supports energetic well-being. Self-compassion is crucial. Recognize that energetic imbalances are a natural part of life, and approach them with kindness and understanding, rather than self-criticism. Practice forgiveness – both of yourself and others – as unresolved emotional issues can significantly impact your energy field. Cultivate gratitude, focusing on the positive aspects of your life, as this enhances positive energy flow. Self-love and self-acceptance are paramount for maintaining a strong and resilient energy field. You must value yourself and treat yourself with the same care and kindness that you would offer to a beloved friend.

Remember, your personal energy field is not separate from the universal energy field; it's an integral part of it.

By strengthening and harmonizing your personal energy field, you are also enhancing your connection to the vast, life-giving energy of the universe. This deeper connection allows for greater clarity, intuition, and access to your innate wisdom. You become more attuned to the subtle currents of life, enabling you to navigate challenges with greater grace and resilience. You also become a more powerful conduit for positive change, radiating your enhanced energy to those around you.

The journey of harnessing your personal energy field is an ongoing exploration. Experiment with different techniques, find what resonates most with you, and adapt your practice as needed. Pay attention to your body's wisdom; it will guide you towards what you need. This path is unique to each individual. Be patient, persistent, and compassionate with yourself throughout the process.

The rewards of cultivating a strong, vibrant energy field are immeasurable, leading to enhanced well-being, spiritual growth, and a deeper connection with the universe's boundless energy. This energetic evolution is a journey of self-discovery, a continuous unfolding of your true potential, and a deeper alignment with your purpose in the grand tapestry of existence. Embrace the process, enjoy the journey, and allow your inner light to shine brightly.

ENERGY HEALING
TECHNIQUES

Having established the foundation of understanding and managing your personal energy field, let's now explore specific energy healing techniques that can significantly enhance your well-being and connection to universal energy. These practices are particularly relevant for Starseeds, who often possess heightened sensitivities and may experience energy imbalances more acutely. This heightened sensitivity, while sometimes challenging, is also a gift, allowing for a deeper perception of the subtle energetic currents that shape our reality.

One of the most widely practiced and accessible energy healing modalities is **Reiki**.

Reiki is a Japanese technique for stress reduction and relaxation that promotes healing. It involves the practitioner channeling universal life force energy through their hands to the recipient. This energy flows to wherever it's needed most, clearing blockages, promoting balance, and facilitating the body's natural healing processes. The experience is often described as deeply relaxing and profoundly restorative, leaving the recipient feeling revitalized and centered. The gentle, non-invasive nature of Reiki makes it suitable for individuals of all ages and health conditions. While receiving Reiki from a qualified practitioner is highly beneficial, there are also self-Reiki techniques you can learn to practice at home, allowing you to support your energetic well-being independently.

Chakra balancing is another fundamental energy healing technique. Chakras are energy centers located along the spine, each associated with specific aspects of your physical, emotional, and spiritual well-being. When your chakras are balanced and flowing freely, your energy system is harmonious, and you experience a sense of overall well-being. However, imbalances can manifest as physical or emotional symptoms, reflecting blockages in the energy flow.

Chakra balancing techniques involve various practices, including meditation, visualization, breathwork, and the use of crystals to restore the natural flow of energy within each chakra. Learning to identify and address imbalances in your chakras can significantly enhance your energetic health and overall sense of well-being.

Many guided meditations are specifically designed to help you balance your chakras; these can be a valuable tool for independent practice.

Energy clearing practices are crucial for removing stagnant or negative energy from your aura and energy field. This is especially important for Starseeds who may be particularly sensitive to external energies. Negative energies can accumulate from various sources, including stressful environments, negative thoughts, and interactions with others. Energy clearing practices can involve various methods, including visualization, smudging with sage or other cleansing herbs, and the use of specific crystals known for their purifying properties. Visualization techniques involve mentally picturing a cleansing light or energy washing over your aura, dissolving and removing any stagnant or negative energies.

Smudging involves burning sage or other cleansing herbs and allowing the smoke to purify your space and aura, creating a clear energetic environment.

Crystals such as selenite and clear quartz are known for their powerful cleansing properties and can be used to enhance energy clearing practices.

Grounding and protection techniques are vital for Starseeds, who often have a strong connection to the universal energy field but might find themselves easily overwhelmed by external energies.

Grounding helps to anchor your energy to the earth, providing stability and preventing energy leaks. This can involve spending time in nature, walking barefoot on the earth, or engaging in grounding meditations that connect you to the earth's stabilizing energy. Protection techniques help to shield your aura from unwanted external energies, preventing them from impacting your emotional and energetic state. This can involve visualization techniques, creating a protective energy field around yourself, or using protective crystals, such as black tourmaline or obsidian. The combination of grounding and protection techniques creates a supportive energetic environment, allowing you to connect with universal energy while maintaining a sense of safety and equilibrium.

Self-healing is an invaluable aspect of managing your energy. Regular meditation, mindful movement, and conscious breathing practices support energetic balance. Guided meditations, specifically designed for self-healing and energy clearing, can be exceptionally powerful tools. Many such meditations are available online or through meditation apps. These guided meditations can lead you through visualizations of cleansing your aura, balancing your chakras, and connecting with universal energy. Consistent practice enhances your energetic awareness and ability to self-regulate your energy flow. Mindful movement, such as yoga or tai chi, can gently clear energetic blockages and promote a sense of flow and balance. Conscious breathing practices, such as deep abdominal breathing or pranayama techniques, can calm your nervous system and facilitate a harmonious flow of energy throughout your body.

The journey of energy healing is a personal one; experiment with different techniques, discover what resonates most deeply with you, and adapt your practices as you grow. Remember, this is a continuous process of self-discovery, requiring patience, persistence, and self-compassion. Track your progress, journal your experiences, and celebrate your successes along the way. Celebrate the small victories and acknowledge the challenges; both are part of the path.

Energy healing is not just about resolving imbalances; it's about deepening your connection with your inner self, your intuition, and the boundless universal energy that flows through all of creation. As you develop your skills in energy healing, you not only improve your own well-being but also become a more potent conduit for positive energy, radiating your enhanced energy to the world around you, creating a ripple effect of healing and transformation. The journey continues, and the universe supports you every step of the way. Embrace the process, trust your intuition, and allow your inner light to shine brightly.

CONNECTING
With Nature's Energy

Having explored various energy healing techniques and the importance of self-healing, we now turn our attention to a profoundly powerful source of universal energy: nature itself. For Starseeds, with their often heightened sensitivity and innate connection to the cosmos, the earth offers a vital grounding and replenishing force. Engaging with the natural world is not merely a pleasant pastime; it's a crucial practice for maintaining energetic balance, enhancing spiritual growth, and deepening the connection to the universal flow.

The earth, in its vastness and complexity, pulsates with a life force that resonates deeply with our own. Trees, mountains, rivers, oceans – each element holds a unique energetic signature, offering a diverse palette of vibrational frequencies to interact with. This interaction is not simply a passive observation; it's an active exchange, a communion between your personal energy field and the boundless energy of the planet. As you spend time in nature, you allow yourself to be immersed in this energetic bath, absorbing its rejuvenating qualities, and releasing stagnant or negative energies that may be weighing you down.

One powerful method of connecting with nature's energy is forest bathing, also known as **shinrin-yoku**. This Japanese practice involves spending time in a forest, immersing yourself in the sights, sounds, smells, and textures of the natural environment. It's not about hiking or achieving a specific goal; it's about slowing down, becoming fully present, and allowing yourself to be enveloped by the forest's restorative atmosphere. As you walk slowly through the woods, notice the subtle nuances of your surroundings – the dappled sunlight filtering through the leaves, the rustling of the wind in the branches, the scent of pine needles and damp earth. Engage all your senses, allowing yourself to be completely absorbed in the moment.

The therapeutic benefits of forest bathing are well-documented.

Studies have shown that spending time in nature lowers blood pressure, reduces stress hormones, and boosts the immune system.

But the benefits extend far beyond the physical realm. Forest bathing provides a profound opportunity for energetic cleansing and rejuvenation. The earth's energy acts as a natural grounding force, anchoring your energy to the planet and preventing energy leaks. The negative ions present in forests are believed to have a positive impact on mood and overall well-being, promoting a sense of calm and tranquility. As you breathe in the fresh forest air, you're not only replenishing your oxygen supply but also absorbing the vital life force energy that permeates the natural world.

Energy work in natural settings offers another avenue for connecting with the earth's energy. You can enhance the effectiveness of your energy healing practices by performing them outdoors. Imagine performing a chakra balancing meditation beneath a towering oak tree, feeling the ancient energy of the tree flow into you, supporting the balance and alignment of your energy centers. Or visualize performing Reiki in a meadow, allowing the sun's energy to amplify the healing power of the universal life force. Nature itself acts as an amplifier, intensifying the energy flow and facilitating deeper healing and transformation. The earth's energy is not just a passive backdrop; it is an active participant in your healing process, providing support and enhancement to your efforts.

Mindful nature walks are a simple yet powerful way to connect with the earth's energy. Instead of rushing through your walk, approach it with intention and presence. Pay attention to the sensations beneath your feet – the texture of the earth, the coolness of the grass, the warmth of the sun on your skin. Notice the sounds surrounding you – the chirping of birds, the rustling of leaves, the gentle murmur of a stream. Engage all your senses, slowing down your pace and allowing yourself to become fully present in the moment. As you walk, imagine roots extending from your feet, grounding you to the earth and drawing up the earth's stabilizing energy.

The practice of consciously connecting with nature's energy is not merely about personal benefit; it's also about cultivating a deep respect and appreciation for the natural world. We are intrinsically connected to the planet, and our well-being is inextricably linked to the health of the environment. By engaging with nature consciously, we foster a sense of responsibility and stewardship towards the earth and its inhabitants. This includes not only respecting the natural beauty of our surroundings but also actively participating in its preservation. Our connection with nature is a reciprocal one; as we draw strength and energy from the earth, we also have a responsibility to give back, protecting and nurturing this precious resource for generations to come. This mindful approach allows for a deeper, more resonant interaction with nature's energy and amplifies the transformative potential of this connection.

The healing properties of nature aren't limited to forests and meadows. Even a small patch of green, a city park, or a rooftop garden can provide a space to connect with the earth's energy. Find spaces in your immediate environment that resonate with you, places where you feel a sense of peace and connection. Regularly visit these spaces, allowing yourself to be present and absorb the healing energy of the natural world. Even simply observing a sunrise or sunset can be a powerful way to connect with the universal energy, reminding us of the cyclical nature of life and the continuous flow of energy that pervades all of creation.

The earth's energy is not a fleeting resource to be exploited; it is a living, breathing entity that responds to our intention and respect.

Approach your interactions with nature with reverence and gratitude, acknowledging the profound gift it offers. Engage in practices that support the health of the environment, such as reducing your carbon footprint, conserving water, and supporting sustainable practices. By integrating conscious engagement with nature into your daily life, you create a positive feedback loop, enhancing not only your personal energetic well-being but also the well-being of the planet itself. This holistic approach fosters a deeper connection with the universal energy, recognizing the interconnectedness of all living things. The earth, in all its magnificence, offers an infinite source of energy, wisdom, and healing – a gift to be cherished and nurtured for generations to come. Embrace this potent connection; it is a fundamental aspect of your Starseed journey and your ongoing evolution.

ECHOES OF THE STARS
Understanding Past Life Lessons from Other Star Systems

The concept of past lives, once confined to the realm of esoteric belief, is increasingly finding resonance with individuals seeking deeper understanding of their present circumstances. While traditional reincarnation focuses on earthly existences, the exciting and expansive notion of past lives in other star systems offers a compelling framework for interpreting current challenges and opportunities. By considering the possibility of prior experiences beyond Earth, we can unlock valuable insights into our karmic imprints, soul evolution, and the unique purpose we carry within this lifetime.

The core principle behind past life lessons, regardless of their extraterrestrial origin, lies in the cyclical nature of experience. We learn and grow through various incarnations, each life presenting specific challenges and opportunities designed to refine our souls and bring us closer to enlightenment. These experiences leave imprints on our subconscious, influencing our tendencies, fears, talents, and relationships. Acknowledging the possibility of past lives in other star systems expands the potential scope of these imprints, suggesting that the challenges we face today may stem from cosmic dramas enacted across the vast expanse of the universe.

One crucial way past life experiences in other star systems can illuminate our current lives is by shedding light on unexplained anxieties and phobias. For instance, a persistent fear of enclosed spaces might not simply be a psychological anomaly but could be a residue from a past life spent trapped on a dying spaceship, or imprisoned within a technologically advanced but oppressive society. Similarly, an aversion to certain technologies or a deep distrust of authority figures could be rooted in experiences on planets where these elements were used for control and subjugation. By exploring these anxieties through techniques like past life regression or intuitive readings, we can begin to understand their origins and integrate the associated trauma, freeing ourselves from their grip.

Furthermore, recognizing past life connections to other star systems can provide context for our inherent talents and passions. A profound aptitude for mathematics and physics, beyond what is explained by our Earthly education, might stem from a past life as a scientist or engineer on a technologically advanced planet. A deep connection to nature and a profound understanding of ecological systems could be a legacy from a life spent as a guardian of a planet's delicate ecosystem. Understanding these past life skills can empower us to embrace our true potential and contribute meaningfully to the world around us.

However, perhaps the most significant benefit of exploring past lives in other star systems lies in the understanding of our karmic relationships. We are often drawn to certain individuals for reasons that are difficult to articulate. These attractions and repulsions may be echoes of past life interactions, offering opportunities to heal old wounds and resolve unfinished business. Recognizing that a difficult relationship might be a karmic debt from a past life on another planet allows us to approach it with compassion and understanding, fostering forgiveness and ultimately, spiritual growth.

Of course, the exploration of past lives in other star systems is inherently speculative and requires a degree of open-mindedness and discernment. It is crucial to approach this topic with a critical yet receptive mindset, avoiding the trap of fantastical narratives and focusing on the underlying lessons and personal growth opportunities. The value lies not in proving the existence of past lives definitively, but in utilizing this framework as a tool for self-discovery and healing.

Considering the possibility of past life experiences in other star systems offers a powerful lens through which to examine our current challenges and opportunities. By exploring the potential origins of our anxieties, talents, and relationships, we can gain a deeper understanding of our soul's journey and unlock the potential for greater self-awareness, healing, and fulfillment. While the mysteries of the universe may remain vast and enigmatic, the echoes of the stars within us can guide us towards a brighter, more purposeful future. The key is to listen, to explore, and to embrace the possibility that our story extends far beyond the confines of this earthly existence.

INTEGRATING
Energy Work into Daily Life

Integrating energy work into the fabric of daily life is not about adding another task to an already overflowing to-do list; it's about subtly shifting the lens through which you perceive and interact with the world. It's about weaving energetic awareness into the very essence of your being, transforming mundane activities into opportunities for growth and connection. This transformation requires intentionality, consistency, and a deep understanding of self-care—the cornerstone of any sustained spiritual practice.

The first step in successfully integrating energy work is recognizing the importance of consistency. Think of it like tending a garden: a single act of planting won't yield a bountiful harvest. Similarly, sporadic bursts of energy work, however powerful, won't yield the same transformative results as regular, consistent practice. Start small. Perhaps five minutes of grounding meditation each morning, or a brief energy clearing before bed. The key is to establish a routine that you can realistically maintain. As you become more comfortable, you can gradually increase the duration and intensity of your practice. The goal isn't to achieve perfection but to cultivate a consistent habit that supports your overall well-being.

Self-care is inextricably linked to the success of any energy practice.

Energy work, especially for Starseeds with their heightened sensitivity, can be energetically demanding. Without adequate self-care, you risk depleting your energy reserves, leading to burnout and hindering your spiritual progress. Self-care is not selfish; it's essential. Prioritize sufficient sleep, nourishment, hydration, and physical activity. Engage in activities that bring you joy and replenish your spirit—spending time in nature, listening to music, engaging in creative pursuits, or simply relaxing and allowing yourself to rest. These seemingly simple practices are crucial for maintaining energetic balance and preventing depletion.

Creating a supportive environment is crucial for fostering a consistent and effective energy work practice. This involves creating a sanctuary, a space where you can retreat and focus without distractions. This doesn't necessarily require a dedicated room; it could be a quiet corner in your home, a comfortable chair in your garden, or even a quiet space in a natural setting. The important thing is that it's a place where you feel safe, comfortable, and free from interruptions. Consider using aromatherapy, crystals, or other sensory elements to enhance the atmosphere and promote relaxation and focus. The goal is to create an environment that supports your energetic well-being and facilitates a deeper connection with your inner self and the universal energy.

Intention-setting is a fundamental aspect of effective energy work. Before beginning any practice, clearly define your intention. What are you hoping to achieve? Are you seeking to clear negative energy, enhance your creativity, improve your physical health, or deepen your spiritual connection? By setting a clear intention, you focus your energy and enhance the effectiveness of your practice. Your intention acts as a guiding force, directing the energy flow towards your desired outcome. It is crucial to approach your practice with a clear mind and an open heart, allowing the universal energy to flow through you unimpeded.

Mindfulness is the key to unlocking the transformative power of energy work. It's about being fully present in the moment, without judgment or expectation. During your energy practices, pay close attention to your physical sensations, emotions, and thoughts. Notice the subtle energy shifts within your body and around you.

Don't get caught up in your thoughts or worries; simply observe them without engaging with them. Allow yourself to be fully present in the experience, allowing the energy to flow naturally without resistance. Mindfulness enhances your awareness, enabling you to fully appreciate the subtle energies that are constantly at play.

Incorporating energy work into daily routines requires a mindful approach. Start by integrating simple practices into your existing schedule. For instance, you can incorporate grounding techniques throughout your day, connecting to the earth's energy by standing barefoot on the ground or focusing on your breath. You can incorporate energy clearing before and after interacting with others or engaging in stressful activities. You can also incorporate brief periods of meditation or visualization throughout your day, using these moments to connect with your inner self and the universal energy. The key is to find small, manageable practices that you can realistically integrate into your daily life without feeling overwhelmed.

Maintaining balance and well-being is paramount when incorporating energy work into daily life. Avoid overdoing it; remember that energy work is a journey, not a race. If you find yourself feeling drained or overwhelmed, take a break and prioritize self-care. Listen to your body's signals and adjust your practice accordingly. Don't be afraid to experiment with different techniques and find what works best for you. Remember, the goal is not to perfectly master energy work but to create a sustainable practice that supports your overall well-being.

Let's dive into some practical strategies for integrating energy work into daily life. Begin your day with a short meditation to set your intention for the day.

- ❖ Visualize yourself filled with positive energy, ready to face challenges with grace and resilience. Throughout the day, take short breaks to ground yourself - connect with the earth's energy by focusing on your breath or placing your feet on the ground. Before engaging in stressful situations or interactions, perform a brief energy clearing. Imagine a protective shield of light surrounding you, deflecting negative energies. At the end of the day, take some time to reflect on your experiences and release any lingering negative energy. Express gratitude for the day's blessings and visualize yourself sleeping peacefully, recharging and rejuvenating.

- ❖ One effective method is to integrate energy work into existing routines. While brushing your teeth, focus on your breath and visualize cleansing energy flowing through your body. During your commute, practice mindfulness by focusing on your senses—the sights, sounds, and feelings around you. While waiting in line, engage in a brief self-healing visualization, focusing on restoring balance to your energy centers. The key is to be creative and find ways to incorporate energy work seamlessly into your daily life.

- ❖ The practice of conscious breathing is a fundamental aspect of energy work, readily integrable into daily routines. Deep, conscious breathing serves as a powerful grounding technique, helping to center and balance your energy. By focusing on your breath, you become more present in the moment, calming your mind and body.

Try practicing deep, diaphragmatic breathing several times throughout the day. Inhale deeply, filling your lungs with air, and exhale slowly, releasing tension and stress. Conscious breathing can be easily integrated into moments of stress, helping you to regain your composure and focus. It can also be used as a transition between activities, creating a sense of calm and centeredness.

Energy work is not just about formal practices; it's about cultivating a state of energetic awareness throughout your day. Pay attention to your energy levels and learn to recognize the signs of energy depletion—fatigue, irritability, anxiety, or feelings of overwhelm.

When you notice these signs, take a break, ground yourself, and practice self-care. By developing your energetic awareness, you learn to proactively manage your energy levels, preventing burnout and maintaining a state of balance. It's about consciously choosing to prioritize your well-being, recognizing your energy as a precious resource to be nurtured and protected.

Integrating energy work into daily life is a transformative process that requires commitment, consistency, and self-compassion. By incorporating simple practices into your daily routines and developing a mindful awareness of your energy levels, you can cultivate a sustainable practice that supports your overall well-being. Remember that the journey is about progress, not perfection. Be patient with yourself, celebrate your successes, and embrace the transformative power of energy work as you embark on your Starseed journey. The ability to consciously manage and utilize your energy is a key element of your unique path, empowering you to navigate the challenges of life with resilience, grace, and a deep connection to the universal energy that flows through all of creation. The universe itself supports this process, ready to amplify your efforts as you align your intention with the natural flow of universal energy. Embrace this journey of self-discovery and allow your innate Starseed wisdom to guide you.

UNCOVERING YOUR STARSEED MISSION

A Cosmic Blueprint for Purpose and Light

So far we acknowledged that the concept of Starseeds offers a compelling narrative for those seeking deeper meaning and purpose in their lives. While the idea might seem fantastical, it resonates with many who feel a profound connection to the cosmos and a burning desire to contribute to a better world. Uncovering one's Starseed mission is a journey of self-discovery, involving the identification of unique gifts, the alignment with one's soul purpose, the understanding of lightworker roles, and the conscious manifestation of a life filled with joy, abundance, and contribution.

One of the initial steps in this journey is recognizing and embracing your unique gifts and talents. We explored the facts that Starseeds are often believed to carry specific skills and knowledge from their past lives, waiting to be awakened and utilized in their current incarnation. These talents might manifest as a natural affinity for healing, a profound understanding of technology, an artistic flair that captivates and inspires, or an innate ability to connect with others on a deep, empathetic level. Identifying these abilities is crucial, as they are often the building blocks for fulfilling one's Starseed mission. Reflecting on Childhood passions, skills that come effortlessly, and subjects that ignite a sense of purpose can provide valuable clues. The key is to move beyond societal expectations and embrace the intrinsic qualities that make you uniquely you, and consider how those qualities can contribute to the collective good, whether through art, innovation, healing, or simply spreading compassion.

However, merely possessing these gifts is not enough; true fulfillment lies in aligning your actions with your soul's purpose. This is the essence of soul alignment, a process of living in accordance with your core values and making choices that resonate with your inner truth. It requires introspection, honest self-assessment, and a willingness to let go of limiting beliefs and societal conditioning.

When aligned with your soul's purpose, life flows with greater ease, synchronicities abound, and a deep sense of peace permeates your being.

This alignment often involves confronting fears, stepping outside your comfort zone, and choosing the path that feels authentic, even when it's challenging or unconventional. This commitment to living authentically empowers you to contribute your unique gifts to the world in a way that is both fulfilling and impactful.

For many Starseeds, the concept of serving as a Lightworker forms a central tenet of their mission. Lightworkers are individuals who have consciously chosen to radiate light and positivity into the world, counteracting negativity and darkness. They do this through various means, including healing, teaching, writing, art, activism, and simply by embodying compassion and kindness in their daily interactions. Understanding the role of Lightworkers involves recognizing the interconnectedness of all beings and the power of collective consciousness. By raising their own vibration and inspiring others to do the same, Lightworkers contribute to the overall ascension of the planet, fostering a world of greater love, peace, and harmony. This service is not about grand gestures; it's about consistently choosing love over fear, hope over despair, and action over apathy.

Ultimately, understanding your Starseed knowledge and intuition can be harnessed to manifest your dreams and create a life of joy, abundance, and purpose. Conscious manifestation is not about wishful thinking; it's about aligning your thoughts, feelings, and actions with the reality you desire. By focusing on positive outcomes, visualizing your goals, and taking inspired action, you can co-create your life with the universe. Your Starseed knowledge and intuition can provide guidance on how to best utilize your gifts, serve the collective good, and attract the resources and opportunities needed to manifest your vision. This process requires patience, perseverance, and unwavering faith in your own abilities and the abundance of the universe.

Uncovering your Starseed mission is a profound journey of self-discovery and empowerment.

By identifying your unique gifts, aligning with your soul's purpose, understanding the role of Lightworkers, and harnessing the power of conscious manifestation, you can create a life filled with joy, abundance, and purpose, while contributing to the collective ascension of humanity. The universe is calling upon those who feel a deep connection to the cosmos to step into their power and embrace their unique roles in creating a brighter future for all. By answering this call, you not only fulfill your own individual mission but also contribute to the healing and transformation of the entire planet.

DISCOVERING
Your Life Purpose

The journey of a Starseed is inherently one of purpose. While the heightened sensitivity and intuitive abilities often associated with this path can bring unique challenges, they also bestow extraordinary gifts—gifts that hold the key to unlocking your unique life purpose. This purpose isn't merely a career path or a checklist of achievements; it's the resonant chord that vibrates at the core of your being, a deep-seated calling that aligns your individual essence with the universal flow of energy.

Discovering this purpose requires introspection, a willingness to delve into the depths of your soul, and a trust in the inherent wisdom that resides within you. It's a journey of self-discovery, one that unfolds organically through self-reflection and attentive listening to the subtle whispers of your intuition. There is no single, prescribed method; the path is unique to each individual, just as your purpose is unique to you.

One powerful tool for self-reflection is journaling. Set aside a dedicated time and space, free from distractions, where you can connect with your inner self. Begin by simply allowing your thoughts and feelings to flow onto the page, without judgment or censorship. Ask yourself open-ended questions: What truly excites me? What activities make me feel most alive? What are my deepest passions and talents? Don't overthink your responses; let the words emerge organically from the wellspring of your subconscious.

Consider keeping a gratitude journal in conjunction with this process. *By focusing on the positive aspects of your life, you create a space for appreciation and allow yourself to see the blessings already present in your life.* Often, our purpose is interwoven with our strengths and passions, things we may take for granted or fail to recognize as gifts. Actively reflecting on what you're grateful for can reveal valuable insights into your unique contributions to the world.

Meditation can be another profoundly effective tool in this journey. Through quiet contemplation, you can silence the noise of the external world and tune into the subtle vibrations of your inner wisdom. Find a comfortable and quiet space, close your eyes, and focus on your breath. As you breathe, visualize yourself as a conduit for universal energy, a channel through which divine guidance flows. Ask yourself questions about your purpose, allowing the answers to emerge naturally from within. Trust the intuitive nudges and insights that arise during your meditative practice. They may appear as fleeting thoughts, images, or sensations – listen carefully to their subtle whispers.

Beyond journaling and meditation, consider engaging your intuition directly. ***Intuition is often described as that inner knowing, a gut feeling or a hunch that guides you towards the right path.*** This is particularly relevant for Starseeds, whose heightened sensitivity often amplifies their intuitive abilities. Pay attention to the recurring themes and synchronicities in your life. These are not mere coincidences but gentle nudges from the universe, guiding you towards your destined path. Trust the whispers of your intuition and allow them to shape your decisions. If a particular idea or opportunity repeatedly presents itself, it may be a sign that you are meant to pursue it.

Once you begin to identify potential paths aligned with your purpose, it's crucial to explore your talents and skills objectively.

These are the instruments through which you will manifest your purpose in the world. Reflect on your past experiences and achievements. What skills have you developed? What challenges have you overcome? What are your natural strengths and abilities? These abilities, honed over lifetimes, are not mere coincidences, but integral aspects of your unique contribution to the collective energy. Understanding your talents and how you can best utilize them is crucial for aligning your actions with your purpose.

As you uncover your talents and passions, consider how they can be applied to make a positive impact on the world. ***For Starseeds, this sense of purpose often extends beyond personal fulfillment; it's deeply connected to the collective good.*** How can your gifts and skills benefit others? Are there causes or communities you feel drawn to? Exploring these questions allows you to connect your purpose to a larger, more meaningful context, reinforcing your commitment and providing a sense of fulfillment that goes beyond personal gain. This larger context provides the necessary framework for a significant, lasting contribution to the world.

Aligning your actions with your discovered purpose is a continual process, not a single event. It requires commitment, intentionality, and a willingness to step outside your comfort zone. Set realistic goals and create actionable steps to move towards your purpose. Celebrate your successes, learn from your setbacks, and maintain a mindset of continuous growth and refinement. Remember that your purpose may evolve and adapt over time, as you grow and learn.

This evolution is a natural part of the process, reflecting your ongoing journey of self-discovery and your continual integration of universal energies.

The path to discovering and fulfilling your life purpose is a journey of self-discovery, guided by intuition and reinforced by conscious action. By embracing self-reflection, exploring your innate talents, and actively aligning your actions with your purpose, you transform from a passive observer of life into an active participant in the unfolding cosmic drama. You become a beacon of light, a powerful force for positive change, manifesting your unique purpose in the world – a purpose deeply interwoven with your Starseed essence and the universal energy that flows through all creation. Embrace this unique journey, for it is within this process that you discover not only your individual purpose, but also the profound interconnectedness that binds you to the universe.

This understanding is not merely an intellectual concept; it is a lived experience, a deeply felt connection that transforms your perception of yourself and your place within the grand tapestry of existence. It's a journey of constant evolution, a dance between your individual aspirations and the universal currents that shape your destiny. *Each step you take, each choice you make, contributes to the unfolding of your unique purpose – a purpose that resonates not only within you but also within the collective consciousness, contributing to the harmonious evolution of all creation.* Embrace the challenges, celebrate the victories, and trust in the inherent wisdom that guides your journey. Your purpose is waiting to be unveiled, ready to illuminate your path and guide you towards a life of profound meaning and fulfillment. The universe, in its infinite wisdom, supports your journey, ready to amplify your efforts as you align yourself with the natural flow of universal energy.

The process of aligning with your purpose is an ongoing dialogue between your inner wisdom and the external world. It's a continuous cycle of reflection, action, and refinement. This isn't a race to the finish line; it's a journey of self-discovery, a dance between intention and unfolding reality. As you move forward, be open to adjustments and changes, always listening to the whispers of your intuition. Your purpose is not a static destination, but a dynamic process of growth and evolution, reflecting the ever-changing landscape of your life and the universe itself.

One significant aspect of aligning with your purpose involves cultivating self-compassion. This is not a journey for the faint of heart; it requires courage, resilience, and a willingness to confront your fears and insecurities. During this process, you may encounter moments of doubt and self-criticism. These are natural parts of the journey, and it's crucial to approach them with kindness and understanding. Treat yourself with the same empathy and compassion that you would offer a close friend facing similar challenges. Remember that the journey of self-discovery is not always linear; it's filled with twists and turns, moments of triumph and setbacks. Self-compassion allows you to navigate these challenges with grace and resilience, ensuring that you emerge stronger and more aligned with your purpose.

Remember, this is your unique journey, and there is no right or wrong way to approach it. Embrace your individuality, trust your intuition, and allow yourself the space to explore and discover your unique path. The universe supports your endeavors, ready to guide you towards a life of purpose and fulfillment. Allow yourself to be a vessel for this universal energy, and watch as your life unfolds in ways you never thought possible. This is your time to shine, your opportunity to make your mark on the world, leaving a legacy that will inspire generations to come. Your journey is not only for your personal growth; it's for the benefit of all creation. Embrace the magnificence of your Starseed journey.

OVERCOMING
Limiting Beliefs

The path to embracing your unique purpose, particularly for Starseeds with their inherent sensitivity and intuitive gifts, is often paved with both exhilarating breakthroughs and challenging obstacles. One of the most significant hurdles on this journey involves confronting and overcoming limiting beliefs. These deeply ingrained patterns of negative self-talk and self-doubt act as invisible barriers, preventing us from accessing our full potential and manifesting our truest selves. They whisper insidious doubts, convincing us we are not capable, not worthy, or simply not meant for the greatness that lies within.

These limiting beliefs aren't simply fleeting thoughts; they are deeply rooted convictions that shape our perception of reality, influencing our choices, actions, and ultimately, our life experiences.

For Starseeds, whose heightened sensitivity often makes them more susceptible to external energies and influences, these limiting beliefs can be particularly potent, hindering their ability to connect with their innate wisdom and manifest their unique purpose. They may manifest as feelings of inadequacy, self-criticism, fear of failure, or a pervasive sense of unworthiness.

These negative thought patterns can create a self-fulfilling prophecy, preventing us from taking the necessary steps towards fulfilling our potential.

Identifying these limiting beliefs is the first crucial step toward overcoming them. Often, these beliefs are deeply ingrained, operating on a subconscious level. They may have originated in Childhood, formed from experiences of criticism, rejection, or trauma. They may also stem from societal conditioning, internalized prejudices, or negative messages absorbed from the environment. To uncover these hidden beliefs, engage in introspective practices such as journaling and meditation. Ask yourself probing questions: What are the recurring negative thoughts that plague my mind?

What are my deepest fears and insecurities?

What are the self-limiting statements I habitually tell myself?

Writing provides a safe space to explore these questions without judgment. Write freely, allowing your thoughts and feelings to flow onto the page. Don't censor yourself; let the words emerge organically, revealing the hidden narratives that shape your perception of yourself and your capabilities. Pay close attention to recurring themes and patterns in your writing. These repetitive thoughts often point towards the core limiting beliefs that are holding you back.

Meditation, with its ability to quiet the mind and connect us to our inner wisdom, offers another powerful tool for identifying limiting beliefs. Through regular practice, you can become more aware of the subtle whispers of your inner critic, recognizing the patterns of negative self-talk and their impact on your emotions and behavior.

As you develop this awareness, you can begin to challenge and dismantle these negative beliefs, replacing them with more empowering and positive affirmations.

Once you've identified your limiting beliefs, the next step involves actively challenging and transforming them. This process requires a shift in perspective, a conscious effort to reframe your thoughts and beliefs. Cognitive reframing involves questioning the validity of these negative beliefs, examining the evidence that supports them, and replacing them with more realistic and empowering alternatives.

For example, if you believe ***"I am not good enough,"*** ask yourself: ***What evidence supports this belief? Are there instances where I have demonstrated competence and success? What qualities and strengths do I possess that contradict this belief?*** By challenging the underlying assumptions of these negative beliefs, you can begin to dismantle their power and replace them with a more positive and realistic self-perception.

Positive affirmations are another powerful tool for overcoming limiting beliefs. These are positive statements that reinforce desired beliefs and counter negative self-talk. They act as a mental rehearsal, programming your subconscious mind with more empowering messages. For example, if you struggle with fear of failure, repeat affirmations such as "I am capable of achieving my goals," or "I embrace challenges as opportunities for growth." Consistency is key in using affirmations; repeat them regularly, ideally both aloud and silently, visualizing the desired outcome as you speak them.

Visualization is a technique often used in New Age practices, and also plays a crucial role in overcoming limiting beliefs. It involves creating mental images of yourself achieving your goals and overcoming obstacles. By vividly visualizing your success, you strengthen your belief in your capabilities and reinforce your commitment to your purpose. The act of visualization aligns your subconscious mind with your conscious intentions, creating a powerful synergy that facilitates the manifestation of your desires.

Self-compassion is very important in this process. Overcoming limiting beliefs is not a quick fix; it's a continuous journey of self-discovery and transformation. There will be setbacks, moments of doubt, and times when you question your progress. It's during these times that self-compassion becomes essential. Treat yourself with the same kindness and understanding you would offer a close friend struggling with similar challenges. Acknowledge your imperfections, celebrate your strengths, and approach your journey with patience and perseverance.

Self-acceptance is inextricably linked to self-compassion. Accepting yourself fully, flaws and all, is crucial for breaking free from the shackles of limiting beliefs. This doesn't mean complacency; it means recognizing your imperfections without judgment, understanding that they are part of your unique and valuable journey. Embrace your vulnerabilities, for they are often the gateways to greater self-awareness and personal growth. This acceptance creates a foundation of self-love, empowering you to move forward with confidence and resilience.

Practical exercises can further enhance the process of releasing limiting beliefs.

- One effective exercise involves writing down your limiting beliefs, then challenging each one with counter-arguments and positive affirmations.

- Another exercise involves creating a vision board that visually represents your goals and aspirations, reinforcing your belief in your ability to achieve them.

- Regular meditation and journaling can also help you track your progress and identify any recurring negative thought patterns.

As we can see, the journey towards overcoming limiting beliefs requires dedication, perseverance, and a commitment to self-growth. But the rewards are immeasurable: a deeper sense of self-awareness, increased self-confidence, and the freedom to embrace your unique purpose and manifest your true potential. Remember, the universe supports your journey, guiding you towards a life of fulfillment and purpose. Embrace the process, trust your intuition, and allow yourself to shine your brightest light.

For Starseeds, this journey is not just about personal growth; it's about fulfilling a cosmic mission, aligning with your unique energy signature, and contributing to the greater good of all creation. Your journey of self-discovery is a testament to the boundless potential within you, a testament waiting to be revealed to the world.

Embrace this journey with open arms, and let your unique light shine brightly.

THE POWER OF
Intention and Manifestation

The journey of self-discovery, particularly for those who identify as Starseeds, often leads to a deeper understanding of the potent connection between intention and manifestation. This isn't about some mystical wish fulfillment; rather, it's about aligning your inner world with the outer, harnessing the power of your focused energy to shape your experience and bring forth your unique purpose.

Think of it as fine-tuning your internal GPS, programming your subconscious mind to navigate towards your desired destination.

Manifestation, at its core, is about creating a resonant frequency between your intention and the universe. It's not about forcing reality to bend to your will, but rather aligning yourself with the natural flow of creation. Just as a radio needs to be tuned to a specific frequency to receive a clear signal, your intention needs to be clear, focused, and unwavering to attract the desired outcomes.

This clarity isn't just about knowing *what* you want; it's about deeply understanding *why* you want it.

The stronger your connection to your "why," the more powerful your manifestation will be. For Starseeds, this "why" often transcends personal desires, encompassing a contribution to the greater good, a healing of the planet, or a fulfillment of a cosmic mission.

Setting intentions involves more than simply making a wish. It requires a conscious and deliberate act of focusing your energy and attention on a specific goal. This begins with self-reflection. Ask yourself: What is my deepest yearning? What contribution do I wish to make to the world? What unique gifts do I bring to the table? The answers to these questions should guide you towards creating intentions that align with your core values and your unique purpose. Don't just focus on the superficial; delve deep into your soul to uncover the authentic desires that fuel your passion and purpose.

Once you've identified your intentions, the next step involves visualizing your desired outcome. This isn't about passively daydreaming; it's about actively engaging your imagination to create a vivid mental picture of your goal already manifested.

Feel the emotions associated with achieving your goal – the joy, the satisfaction, the sense of accomplishment. The more vividly you can visualize and feel the desired outcome, the stronger the energetic imprint you create, attracting the necessary resources and opportunities to bring your intention into reality.

A vision board is a powerful tool for manifesting your intentions by visually representing your goals and aspirations.

Gather images, words, and objects that symbolize your desired outcomes, arranging them on a board to create a dynamic visual representation of your intentions. Place this board where you'll see it regularly, reminding yourself of your goals and keeping your intentions at the forefront of your mind. This consistent visual reminder acts as a constant affirmation, subtly programming your subconscious mind to work towards your desired reality.

Affirmations are another powerful tool in the manifestation process. These are positive statements that reinforce your desired beliefs and counteract negative self-talk. Choose affirmations that resonate deeply with your intentions and repeat them regularly, both silently and aloud. As you speak your affirmations, feel the energy behind your words, fully believing in their truth. The consistent repetition of affirmations reprograms your subconscious mind, replacing limiting beliefs with empowering ones, paving the way for the manifestation of your desires.

For example, if your intention is to connect with your soul purpose, you might use affirmations such as, *"I am aligned with my divine purpose," or "I am guided and supported in fulfilling my life's mission."*

Aligning your intentions with your values is crucial for successful manifestation.

If your intentions are not rooted in your core values, they are likely to lack authenticity and staying power. For instance, if your deepest value is service to others, your intentions should reflect this value – perhaps volunteering your time, starting a non-profit organization, or using your skills to support a cause you believe in. When your intentions are in harmony with your values, your actions will naturally follow, and your manifestation process will flow effortlessly.

The process of manifestation requires consistent effort and dedication. It's about actively engaging with your intentions, regularly practicing visualization and affirmations, and consistently taking steps towards your goals. However, it's also important to remember that the journey of manifestation is not always linear. There may be obstacles and setbacks along the way, moments of doubt and uncertainty. This is where self-compassion and perseverance come into play. Celebrate your successes, learn from your setbacks, and never give up on your dreams.

For Starseeds, the process of manifestation takes on a heightened significance. Your heightened sensitivity and intuitive abilities can amplify your connection to the universe, allowing you to manifest your intentions with greater ease and efficiency. However, this sensitivity can also make you more susceptible to external energies and influences, potentially hindering your manifestation process. It's crucial to protect your energy field, engaging in practices such as meditation, grounding, and energy clearing to shield yourself from negativity and maintain a clear energetic pathway for your intentions to manifest.

Remember, the universe is not a vending machine where you insert an intention and receive an instant reward. The process of manifestation is a collaborative one, requiring your active participation and alignment with the divine flow of creation. Trust in the process, remain steadfast in your intentions, and have unwavering faith in your ability to create the reality you desire.

Your unique purpose awaits, ready to be unveiled through the power of your intention and the magic of manifestation.

The power of intention extends beyond personal desires; it also has the potential to impact the collective consciousness. Starseeds, with their heightened awareness and connection to universal energy, are uniquely positioned to use their intentions to create positive change in the world. By aligning your intentions with the betterment of humanity and the planet, you can contribute to a wave of positive transformation that ripples outwards, affecting countless lives. This is the essence of the Starseed mission – to use your unique gifts and energy to uplift and inspire others, creating a world of harmony, peace, and abundance.

The path to manifesting your unique purpose is not always easy. There will be challenges, obstacles, and moments of doubt.

However, by maintaining a strong connection to your intention, persistently visualizing your desired outcomes, and employing effective manifestation techniques, you can navigate these challenges with grace and resilience. ***Remember that your journey is unique, and the timeline for manifestation varies depending on individual circumstances and energetic alignment.*** Trust in your inner wisdom, embrace your unique gifts, and remain steadfast in your commitment to your purpose.

Cultivating a mindset of gratitude is essential in the manifestation process. By focusing on the positive aspects of your life and expressing gratitude for what you already have, you create a vibrational frequency that attracts more positive experiences and opportunities. Regular gratitude practices, such as journaling about what you are grateful for or expressing appreciation to others, can significantly enhance your ability to manifest your desires. This heightened appreciation doesn't mean ignoring challenges; instead, it involves acknowledging the lessons learned and finding gratitude even amidst difficulty. Gratitude fosters an inner sense of abundance, creating a fertile ground for your intentions to blossom.

Ultimately, the power of intention and manifestation lies in your ability to connect with your inner wisdom, align your thoughts and actions with your purpose, and trust in the universe's support. This is a journey of self-discovery, a path towards realizing your full potential, and fulfilling your unique mission in this lifetime. For Starseeds, this is not just about personal growth; it's about contributing to a larger cosmic plan, using your unique energy signature to create a positive impact on the world and beyond. Embrace the journey, trust the process, and let your unique light shine brightly. Your unique purpose is waiting to unfold, ready to be revealed to the world through the power of your unwavering intention. The universe is listening, ready to assist you in fulfilling your cosmic mission. The stars align, not just for you, but because of you. Your journey is a testament to the boundless possibilities available when intention meets action, when spirit meets reality.

Embrace your power, embrace your purpose, and embrace the magnificence of your being.

Finding Your Tribe

The journey of a Starseed, as we've explored, is one of profound self-discovery, a path illuminated by the unique gifts and heightened sensitivities that often accompany this soul's earthly experience.

However, this journey is rarely undertaken in isolation. Just as a single star shines brighter when surrounded by a constellation, so too does the Starseed's path become richer and more fulfilling when shared with a community of kindred spirits. Finding your tribe –your chosen family of like-minded individuals who understand and support your unique experiences – is paramount to navigating this extraordinary life.

This is not merely about socializing or finding friends; it's about cultivating deep, meaningful connections with individuals who resonate with your soul's purpose, who understand the nuances of your heightened sensitivity and intuitive abilities, and who share a similar understanding of the universe's subtle energies. These connections offer a sense of belonging, a refuge from the potential isolation that can accompany the Starseed experience, and a powerful source of support during challenging times. The shared experiences and mutual understanding within a supportive community can transform the often-solitary journey into a collaborative exploration of consciousness, purpose, and interconnectedness.

The benefits of finding your tribe are manifold. Firstly, it provides a safe space to share your experiences without judgment. The heightened sensitivity of Starseeds often leads to a deeper awareness of the world's complexities, including its pain and suffering. This can be both a gift and a burden. Connecting with others who share this sensitivity allows you to express your emotions, your doubts, and your triumphs without feeling misunderstood or ostracized.

This sense of validation and acceptance is essential for emotional well-being and spiritual growth.

Furthermore, your tribe becomes a wellspring of wisdom and inspiration. Within this community, you'll encounter a diverse range of perspectives, experiences, and practices that can enrich your own understanding of yourself and your purpose. The collective knowledge and insights shared within the group can illuminate your path, offering guidance, support, and encouragement when you face challenges. This shared learning environment fosters mutual growth and a sense of collective responsibility for each other's journey.

Moreover, your tribe can offer invaluable practical support. The Starseed path, while often rewarding, can be demanding. The intensity of your energy, your intuitive abilities, and your sensitivity to external energies can sometimes lead to emotional or energetic exhaustion. In these moments, the support of your tribe is invaluable. They can offer practical advice, emotional support, and energetic assistance, helping you navigate challenging times and regain your balance.

Finding your tribe can be an organic process, unfolding naturally as you connect with others on a soul level. However, it can also require a conscious effort and a willingness to put yourself out there. There are numerous avenues to explore in your search for your community.

Online platforms offer a rich tapestry of opportunities to connect with like-minded individuals. Numerous forums, social media groups, and online communities dedicated to Starseeds, Indigo Children, and other spiritually inclined individuals provide spaces for sharing experiences, exchanging ideas, and building connections. These platforms offer a convenient way to connect with others who may live far away, fostering a sense of global community and expanding your circle of support. However, remember to approach online interactions with discernment and caution, ensuring the platforms you engage with are supportive and respectful.

Offline opportunities also abound. Spiritual retreats, workshops, and conferences are excellent venues for meeting like-minded individuals. These events often provide structured opportunities for interaction, allowing you to share your experiences and connect with others in a more personal and intimate setting. The shared experiences of these events can create powerful bonds, solidifying your connections within your emerging community. Participating in local spiritual or metaphysical groups can also provide opportunities for connection, offering a chance to engage with others in a regular setting and build lasting relationships.

The key to finding your tribe is to remain open, receptive, and authentic. Be true to yourself, share your experiences honestly, and trust your intuition to guide you towards those who resonate with your soul's energy. Don't be afraid to reach out to others, initiate conversations, and build connections. The more you engage with your community, the more you'll discover the richness and support that comes from belonging to a tribe of like-minded souls.

Building a supportive and safe space within your tribe is crucial for mutual growth and well-being. This requires establishing ground rules for interaction, fostering respectful communication, and creating an environment of trust and openness. Clear boundaries are essential to protect everyone's emotional and energetic well-being, ensuring the space remains a refuge and not a source of stress or negativity. Active listening, empathy, and a willingness to support each other through challenges are vital components of a thriving community.

The importance of shared experiences within your tribe cannot be overstated. Whether it's a shared meditation, a collaborative creative project, or simply a conversation over tea, shared experiences strengthen bonds and deepen connections. These shared moments create a sense of belonging, reinforcing the feeling of community and shared purpose. They also provide opportunities for learning, growth, and mutual support.

Remember that finding your tribe is an ongoing process, a journey of discovery and connection. It's not about finding the perfect community, but about cultivating relationships with individuals who support your growth and amplify your light. The journey itself is part of the experience, and the connections you forge will enrich and amplify your Starseed journey, illuminating your path towards your unique purpose and contributing to a more harmonious and enlightened world. Embrace the process, trust your intuition, and allow your community to lift you and support your unique contribution to the collective consciousness. The stars are guiding you, and you are not alone. Your tribe awaits, ready to welcome you home.

Making a Difference
in the World

The journey of self-discovery, as we've seen, is intricately constructed with the threads of connection and community. Finding your tribe, your supportive network of kindred spirits, is essential for navigating the often-intense emotional and energetic landscape of the Starseed experience. But the journey doesn't end with self-understanding; it extends outwards, towards a world yearning for the unique gifts you possess. The heightened sensitivity, the intuitive insights, the potent energy that defines the Starseed path –these are not solely for personal growth; they are potent tools for making a profound difference in the world.

Your unique purpose, as a Starseed, isn't confined to your inner world. It's a call to action, a beckoning to utilize your gifts for the betterment of humanity and the planet. This isn't about grand gestures or achieving worldwide fame; it's about aligning your actions with your values and utilizing your inherent abilities to create positive change, however small it may seem. It's about living a life of purpose, radiating your unique energy into the world, and inspiring others to do the same.

One of the most powerful ways Starseeds can make a difference is through acts of service and volunteering. Your heightened empathy and intuitive understanding allow you to connect deeply with others' suffering, empowering you to offer support and compassion in ways others might not. Volunteering at a local soup kitchen, offering your time at an animal shelter, or assisting the elderly are all ways to channel your energy into tangible acts of kindness. The act of service itself is transformative; it grounds your energy, connects you to the collective human experience, and offers a profound sense of fulfillment that transcends personal gain. The energy exchange in such acts is remarkably powerful, a subtle yet profound alchemy of giving and receiving.

Beyond direct service, consider how your intuitive abilities can guide you towards causes that truly resonate with your soul's purpose. Perhaps you feel a deep connection to environmental conservation, drawn to protect the planet's delicate ecosystems. Or maybe social justice issues ignite a fire within you, prompting you to advocate for the marginalized and oppressed. This inner guidance is invaluable. It helps you focus your efforts, maximizing your impact and ensuring your actions are aligned with your deepest values. Don't underestimate the power of intuition; it's a compass guiding you towards your most authentic and impactful contribution.

Creative expression is another potent avenue for Starseeds to make a difference. The unique perspective and heightened sensitivity often associated with Starseeds translate into extraordinary creative output. Whether it's painting, writing, music, dance, or any other form of artistic expression, your creations have the power to touch hearts, inspire change, and shift collective consciousness. Your art can become a conduit for healing, a vehicle for conveying profound truths, and a bridge connecting individuals to a deeper understanding of themselves and the world around them. Consider the impact of a powerful poem that speaks to the collective grief of a community, or a painting that inspires awe and wonder, reminding viewers of the beauty of the natural world. Your creative energy has the power to transform lives.

Activism, in its many forms, offers another pathway for Starseeds to contribute. Your intuitive abilities can help you identify injustices, pinpoint effective strategies for change, and inspire others to join the movement. Whether you're advocating for environmental protection, social equality, or animal rights, your unique energy can energize and empower others to join the cause. Remember that activism isn't solely about grand public demonstrations; it can also involve small, everyday acts of resistance, such as speaking out against injustice in your community, supporting ethical businesses, or simply choosing to live in accordance with your values. Every act, no matter how small, contributes to the ripple effect of change.

Community service, in its broadest sense, encompasses many of the avenues we've discussed. It involves actively participating in the betterment of your local community, fostering a sense of connection and shared purpose. This might involve organizing community events, mentoring young people, or simply engaging in meaningful conversations with your neighbors. Building strong, supportive communities is paramount, not only for individual well-being but also for creating a more resilient and compassionate world.

It is important to remember that making a difference isn't about seeking external validation or recognition. It's about aligning your actions with your values, honoring your inner guidance, and embracing your unique gifts.

The impact you make may not always be immediately visible, but it's undoubtedly significant. The energy you radiate, the positive changes you initiate, the ripple effect of your actions – these are all part of a larger cosmic tapestry, contributing to a more harmonious and enlightened world.

Think of individuals who have significantly impacted the world, often driven by a deep sense of purpose rooted in their unique sensitivities. Consider environmental activists like Greta Thunberg, whose passionate advocacy resonated with millions and sparked a global movement. Or contemplate the work of artists like Bob Dylan, whose music became a soundtrack to social change, inspiring generations to challenge the status quo. These are just examples of individuals who channeled their unique energies to effect positive transformations, individuals who, in their own ways, embodied the spirit of the Starseed.

Your path, too, is unique. There is no single "right" way to make a difference. The key lies in discovering the ways that feel most authentic and fulfilling to you. Explore different avenues, experiment with various approaches, and trust your intuition to guide you. Don't be afraid to step outside your comfort zone; the most significant growth often occurs when we embrace challenges and venture into uncharted territory.

The journey of a Starseed is a lifelong process of learning, growth, and evolution. It's about continuously refining your understanding of your unique purpose, adapting to the changing landscape of your experiences, and responding to the calls of your soul. This includes actively seeking opportunities to contribute to the greater good, utilizing your gifts to create positive change, and sharing your energy with the world.

The world is in need of your unique contributions. Your heightened sensitivity, your intuitive wisdom, your potent energy – these are not merely personal attributes; they are potent tools for transformation. Embrace your gifts, align your actions with your values, and embark on your journey of making a difference. Your unique purpose awaits, beckoning you to shine your light brightly and illuminate the path for others. Your impact may be subtle at first, a gentle ripple in the vast ocean of humanity, but over time, these ripples will converge, creating waves of positive change that will continue to resonate for generations to come.

Remember that your journey is not solitary. Your tribe, your community of like-minded souls, provides the support, encouragement, and inspiration you need to navigate this path. Lean on your community, share your experiences, and allow their collective energy to amplify your own. Together, we can create a world filled with compassion, understanding, and profound positive change. The universe is calling, your purpose is clear, and the time to act is now.

Embrace your unique gifts!

The world awaits your contribution.

UNDERSTANDING
Sufferings Purpose

Suffering, an unavoidable aspect of the human experience, takes on a unique significance within the Starseed journey. Often characterized by heightened sensitivity and a deep connection to the collective consciousness, Starseeds may find themselves more acutely affected by the world's pain and their own internal struggles. However, this heightened sensitivity isn't a weakness; rather, it's a powerful tool for growth and transformation, a conduit for understanding the deeper purpose behind life's challenges.

Many spiritual traditions view suffering not as punishment or a random occurrence but as a catalyst for spiritual awakening.

Consider the Buddhist concept of dukkha, often translated as suffering, dissatisfaction, or unsatisfactoriness. Dukkha isn't merely physical or emotional pain; it encompasses the inherent impermanence of life, the constant flux of existence that can lead to feelings of anxiety, frustration, and disillusionment. Yet, within the Buddhist framework, confronting dukkha, understanding its nature, and accepting its presence are essential steps on the path to enlightenment. The process of grappling with suffering leads to a deeper understanding of the self, a release from attachment to ephemeral things, and ultimately, a path to liberation.

Similarly, many other spiritual and philosophical traditions see suffering as a teacher, a crucible in which the soul is refined and strengthened. The trials and tribulations we face often force us to confront our deepest fears, beliefs, and limitations. By navigating these challenges, we uncover hidden strengths, develop resilience, and gain a deeper understanding of our own potential for growth.

The process of overcoming adversity builds character, fostering compassion, empathy, and a profound appreciation for the preciousness of life.

From a psychological perspective, suffering can be understood as a signal, an indicator that something within our lives needs attention.

It may be a sign of unmet needs, unresolved trauma, or a misalignment between our values and our actions. *While the experience of suffering is undeniably difficult, it provides valuable feedback, prompting us to examine our lives more deeply and make necessary changes.* This process of self-reflection and adjustment, often facilitated by therapy or other forms of self-help, can lead to significant personal growth and a greater sense of well-being. The pain itself becomes a catalyst for healing, allowing us to process past traumas and develop healthier coping mechanisms.

For Starseeds, the intensity of their emotional and energetic sensitivity can amplify the experience of suffering. They may feel the pain of the world more acutely, experiencing empathy and compassion on a deeper level than many others. This can lead to feelings of overwhelm, burnout, and a sense of responsibility for the world's suffering. While this heightened sensitivity can be challenging, it also presents an opportunity for profound growth and transformation. By embracing their empathy and utilizing their intuitive abilities, Starseeds can channel their energy towards healing and positive change, finding purpose and meaning amidst the pain.

Navigating suffering effectively requires a comprehensive approach, incorporating both spiritual and psychological tools. Mindfulness practices, such as meditation and yoga, can help to cultivate awareness of our thoughts, feelings, and sensations without judgment. This increased awareness allows us to observe our suffering without being overwhelmed by it, creating space for acceptance and understanding. Journaling can also be a powerful tool for processing emotions, identifying patterns, and gaining insight into the root causes of suffering. By writing about our experiences, we can create distance from our emotions, allowing for a more objective perspective.

Developing healthy coping mechanisms is crucial for managing the challenges that inevitably arise. This might involve engaging in activities that bring joy and relaxation, such as spending time in nature, listening to music, or pursuing creative hobbies. It's important to prioritize self-care, ensuring that we are meeting our physical, emotional, and spiritual needs. Building a strong support network of friends, family, and community is also essential. Sharing our experiences with others who understand can provide comfort, validation, and a sense of belonging. This sense of connection is particularly crucial for Starseeds, who may feel isolated or misunderstood due to their heightened sensitivity.

For Starseeds, connecting with their spiritual practices is paramount in navigating suffering. Whether it involves meditation, prayer, energy work, or other forms of spiritual connection, these practices can provide solace, guidance, and a sense of purpose. *It's important to remember that we are not alone in our suffering; we are part of a larger interconnected web of life, and spiritual practices can help us to connect with this larger context, finding strength and comfort in our shared humanity.*

It is also vital to remember that suffering doesn't always require immediate resolution. Sometimes, the process of growth involves embracing the discomfort, allowing ourselves to feel the pain without trying to suppress or escape it. This doesn't mean passively accepting suffering; rather, it means acknowledging its presence and allowing it to guide us towards greater self-awareness and understanding. Sometimes, the most valuable lessons are learned in the depths of our suffering.

The heightened sensitivity often associated with Starseeds can make them acutely aware of the suffering in the world. This awareness can be both a blessing and a challenge. It can inspire them to dedicate their lives to service and activism, working to alleviate suffering and create a more compassionate world. However, it can also lead to feelings of overwhelm and a sense of responsibility that can be difficult to manage. It is essential for Starseeds to find a balance between their compassion and their own well-being, ensuring they don't become consumed by the suffering of others.

Remember that the journey of transformation is not linear; it's a winding path with ups and downs, periods of growth intertwined with moments of stagnation or even regression. It's important to be patient with yourself and to celebrate the small victories along the way. Acknowledge and honor the challenges faced, learning from them rather than allowing them to define you. Every experience, both positive and negative, is an opportunity for growth and evolution.

In the end, ***the purpose of suffering within the Starseed journey is not to inflict pain or to test resilience. Instead, it serves as a powerful catalyst for transformation, a catalyst that pushes boundaries, deepens understanding, and ultimately, propels the Starseed toward fulfilling their unique purpose in the world.*** The pain experienced can become a gateway to profound compassion, enhanced empathy, and a life lived with greater purpose and meaning. Embrace the challenges, learn from the experiences, and allow the suffering to guide you on your transformative journey.

Your inherent strength and resilience will help you navigate the complexities of life and emerge stronger, wiser, and more aligned with your true self. The transformative power lies not in avoiding suffering but in embracing it as a critical component of your growth and evolution. The lessons learned in the crucible of suffering will ultimately serve to illuminate your path and strengthen your resolve to fulfil your unique purpose in this lifetime and beyond.

The universe is unfolding, and you are an essential part of that unfolding.

EMBRACING
Challenges as Opportunities

Embracing challenges, particularly for those who identify as Starseeds, requires a shift in perspective. Instead of viewing difficulties as obstacles to be overcome, we can reframe them as opportunities for profound growth and self-discovery. This isn't about naive optimism; it's about cultivating a resilient mindset that acknowledges the reality of hardship while simultaneously recognizing its potential for positive transformation. This shift involves cultivating several key skills and attitudes.

Mindful Acceptance... One of the most powerful tools is the practice of mindful acceptance. This doesn't mean passively enduring suffering; rather, it involves acknowledging its presence without judgment.

Mindfulness encourages us to observe our thoughts and feelings as they arise, without getting carried away by them. Instead of reacting impulsively to a challenge, we create space for a more considered response. Imagine facing a difficult conversation—mindfulness allows us to observe the rising anxiety, the tightening in our chest, without letting it control our behavior. This creates space for thoughtful communication, rather than a knee-jerk reaction fueled by fear. This mindful acceptance is the foundation upon which resilience is built.

Resilience, in this context, isn't about avoiding challenges; it's about developing the capacity to bounce back from adversity, to learn from setbacks, and to emerge stronger and wiser. This involves cultivating a sense of inner strength, a belief in our ability to navigate difficult situations. This isn't an innate trait; it's a skill that is honed through practice and conscious effort. Developing resilience often involves actively seeking out challenges, viewing them as opportunities to test our limits and discover hidden strengths. Consider a Starseed grappling with feelings of overwhelm due to their heightened sensitivity. Instead of withdrawing from the world, they could consciously choose to engage with their sensitivity in a controlled manner, perhaps through creative expression or acts of service, transforming overwhelm into purposeful action.

Developing effective coping mechanisms is also crucial. These are the strategies we use to manage stress and navigate difficult emotions. For some, this might involve engaging in physical activity—a vigorous workout can be a powerful way to release pent-up energy and alleviate stress. For others, it might involve creative pursuits like painting, writing, or playing music—these activities can provide a healthy outlet for processing emotions and fostering self-expression. Nature provides another potent source of solace. Spending time in natural environments has been shown to reduce stress, improve mood, and promote a sense of well-being. The rhythmic sounds of waves crashing on the shore, the calming presence of a forest, can help restore our equilibrium and provide perspective. The choice of coping mechanism depends on the individual; the key is finding what works best for you, fostering a personal toolkit to navigate stress and emotional difficulties.

Emotional Regulation... Another essential element of embracing challenges as opportunities is the development of emotional regulation. This involves learning to manage our emotional responses in a healthy way, avoiding impulsive reactions that can exacerbate difficult situations.

Techniques such as deep breathing exercises, progressive muscle relaxation, and mindfulness meditation can be incredibly helpful in calming the nervous system and fostering a sense of inner peace.

These practices help us to create distance between our emotions and our actions, allowing us to respond more thoughtfully and effectively to challenges. Learning to identify and label our emotions is also an important aspect of emotional regulation. When we are able to name what we are feeling—anger, sadness, fear—we gain a sense of control over our emotional experience. This self-awareness allows us to choose how we respond to our feelings, rather than reacting impulsively.

Problem-solving skills are another vital aspect of this transformative process. Challenges often require active engagement, thoughtful consideration, and a willingness to explore different solutions. This can involve brainstorming potential solutions, evaluating their feasibility, and choosing the most effective course of action. It often involves breaking down complex problems into smaller, more manageable steps, making the task less daunting and more approachable. Seeking guidance from others can also be beneficial; sharing our challenges with trusted friends, family, or mentors can provide valuable support, perspective, and new ideas. Collaboration is a powerful tool for problem-solving, providing access to diverse perspectives and solutions that we might not have considered independently.

Finding meaning in adversity is perhaps the most significant aspect of this process. This involves seeking a deeper understanding of the purpose behind our challenges, viewing them not as random occurrences but as opportunities for growth and spiritual awakening. This might involve reflecting on the lessons learned from difficult experiences, identifying areas for personal growth, and recognizing the strength and resilience developed through overcoming adversity. Journaling can be a helpful tool in this process, allowing for introspection and reflection. By writing about our experiences, we gain distance from our emotions, creating space for greater understanding and insight.

For Starseeds, the intensity of their experiences often amplifies the need for these strategies. Their heightened sensitivity can make challenges more impactful, requiring a more deliberate approach to self-care and emotional regulation. However, this heightened sensitivity is also a strength—it provides an increased capacity for empathy, compassion, and a deeper understanding of the interconnectedness of life. They often possess unique intuitive abilities that can provide guidance and insight during challenging times. By consciously integrating these abilities into their coping strategies, Starseeds can harness their sensitivity for personal growth and transformation.

The process is never linear; there will be setbacks and moments of doubt. Self-compassion is essential during these times. Treat yourself with the same kindness and understanding that you would offer a friend facing similar challenges. Acknowledge that setbacks are a normal part of the growth process and use them as an opportunity to reassess strategies and refine approaches. The journey is about progress, not perfection, a continuous process of learning and adaptation.

Remember, the universe works in mysterious ways; challenges often appear as obstacles, but in reality, they are invitations to evolve, to discover hidden potential, and to fulfill our unique purpose.

Embrace the process; trust in your inner strength, and know that you are not alone on this transformative journey. The path forward is illuminated by your resilience, your inner wisdom, and the inherent strength residing within your Starseed soul. Embrace the challenges—they are the stepping stones to a more meaningful and fulfilling life, a life aligned with your highest potential. The universe is unfolding, and your journey, with all its complexities and challenges, is a crucial part of that unfolding.

THE PATH TO
Self-Acceptance

The journey towards self-acceptance, especially for those who identify as Starseeds, is a profound and often challenging undertaking. This heightened sensitivity, while a gift, can also amplify feelings of otherness, inadequacy, and a sense of not quite belonging. The path to self-love, however, is not a destination but a continuous unfolding, a process of self-discovery and integration.

One of the foundational elements of this journey is building self-esteem. This isn't about inflated ego or self-aggrandizement; it's about cultivating a realistic and positive view of oneself, recognizing one's strengths, talents, and unique contributions to the world. For Starseeds, this might involve acknowledging their intuitive abilities, their heightened empathy, and their capacity for profound connection with others. It requires a conscious effort to shift focus away from perceived flaws and shortcomings, toward appreciating the inherent worth and value that resides within. This may involve identifying and celebrating past accomplishments, no matter how small. Reflecting on moments where you overcame adversity, demonstrated courage, or showed kindness to others can provide tangible evidence of your self-worth.

Writing can be a powerful tool in this process. By regularly writing down your thoughts and feelings, you can gain a clearer understanding of your inner landscape. Focusing on your strengths, your accomplishments, and the positive qualities that make you unique can help build a more positive self-image. Moreover, writing provides a safe space for self-reflection, allowing you to explore any limiting beliefs or negative self-talk that may be hindering your self-acceptance. Identifying these patterns is the first step towards challenging and overcoming them.

Cultivating self-compassion is another crucial aspect of this journey. Self-compassion involves treating oneself with the same kindness, understanding, and empathy that you would offer a close friend facing similar challenges. It recognizes that everyone makes mistakes, experiences setbacks, and falls short of their own expectations from time to time. This isn't about self-indulgence or ignoring personal responsibility; it's about acknowledging your imperfections with kindness and understanding, rather than self-criticism and judgment. When faced with difficult emotions or self-doubt, practice speaking to yourself with the same compassion and support you would offer a loved one in a similar situation. Imagine offering words of encouragement and understanding to a friend struggling with self-acceptance. Now, offer those same words to yourself.

Self-forgiveness is intrinsically linked to self-compassion. We all carry burdens of past regrets, mistakes, and perceived failures. Holding onto these burdens weighs heavily on our spirits, impeding our ability to move forward and embrace a life of self-acceptance. Self-forgiveness is not about condoning harmful actions; rather, it's about releasing the grip of self-judgment and acknowledging that past actions do not define your present self or future potential. It is about acknowledging the past, learning from it, and consciously choosing to release the emotional weight it carries. This process can be aided by mindful meditation, focusing on the breath and allowing yourself to simply be present in the moment, without judgment.

Mindfulness practices, such as meditation and deep breathing exercises, help to quiet the inner critic and create space for self-compassion. By focusing on the present moment, you can detach from the relentless stream of negative self-talk and cultivate a more balanced perspective. Mindfulness isn't about ignoring your feelings; it's about observing them without judgment. Notice the thoughts and feelings that arise, acknowledge them, and allow them to pass without getting entangled in their emotional grip. Regular practice helps cultivate a sense of inner peace and acceptance, even in the face of challenging emotions.

Self-reflection exercises can further enhance this journey. These exercises involve consciously examining your thoughts, beliefs, and behaviors to identify patterns and limiting beliefs that may be hindering your self-acceptance. This could involve asking yourself questions such as: What are my core values? What are my strengths and weaknesses? What are my limiting beliefs about myself? What stories do I tell myself about my past? Honest introspection can illuminate blind spots and unveil areas where self-compassion and forgiveness are needed. Guided meditations, specifically designed for self-reflection, can be invaluable in this process.

Self-care is not selfish; it is essential for nurturing your physical, emotional, and spiritual well-being. This involves prioritizing activities that nourish your soul and bring you joy. For Starseeds, this might involve spending time in nature, engaging in creative pursuits, connecting with like-minded individuals, or practicing energy healing techniques. It might also involve setting healthy boundaries, learning to say no to commitments that drain your energy, and prioritizing activities that bring you a sense of peace and contentment. Self-care is an act of self-love, a conscious choice to prioritize your well-being.

The concept of **self-image** is crucial. Our self-image is the mental picture we hold of ourselves. It's shaped by our experiences, beliefs, and the messages we receive from others. A negative self-image can significantly hinder self-acceptance. Consciously working to cultivate a more positive and realistic self-image is essential. This involves challenging negative self-talk, replacing critical thoughts with more compassionate and supportive ones. It's about acknowledging your flaws without letting them define you, focusing instead on your strengths and positive qualities.

For Starseeds, the journey toward self-acceptance may require additional attention to their heightened sensitivity. This sensitivity can make them more susceptible to the opinions and energies of others, potentially leading to self-doubt and feelings of inadequacy.

It's crucial for Starseeds to develop strong boundaries, protecting their energy from external influences that might diminish their self-worth. This might involve practicing energetic shielding techniques, surrounding themselves with supportive and uplifting people, and consciously limiting exposure to negative environments or individuals.

Remember, the path to self-acceptance is not linear. There will be ups and downs, moments of self-doubt, and challenges that test your resolve. The key is to approach these moments with self-compassion, acknowledging that setbacks are a normal part of the growth process. Be patient and kind to yourself, recognizing that progress, not perfection, is the goal. Celebrate small victories along the way, and remember that you are not alone on this journey. Many others share your experiences and struggles, and a supportive community can provide invaluable guidance and encouragement.

The universe supports your journey towards self-acceptance; embrace the process and trust in your inherent worth. Your unique Starseed energy holds immense potential for growth and transformation; nurture it, love it, and allow it to guide you toward a life of authentic self-expression and profound inner peace. The journey is worth it; the rewards are beyond measure.

Forgiveness *and* Letting Go

The journey of self-acceptance, as we've explored, is an intimate experience and often a challenging odyssey. It requires courage, self-compassion, and a willingness to confront our inner landscape with honesty and grace. Yet, even with the cultivation of self-love and self-esteem, a significant obstacle can remain: the weight of unforgiveness. Holding onto resentment, anger, and past hurts, whether directed at ourselves or others, creates a heavy emotional burden that impedes our spiritual growth and overall well-being. This section delves into the transformative power of forgiveness –both self-forgiveness and forgiving others – as a crucial element in the healing process.

Unforgiveness acts as a subtle yet potent poison, slowly eroding our inner peace and joy. It manifests not only in obvious anger and bitterness but also in more insidious ways: anxiety, depression, physical ailments, and strained relationships. The emotional energy we expend on harboring resentment is energy that could be channeled towards self-nurturing, creativity, and fulfilling our life's purpose. For Starseeds, with their inherent sensitivity, the impact of unforgiveness can be particularly profound, as they tend to absorb and amplify emotional energies, both their own and those around them.

Self-forgiveness, as discussed earlier, is a foundational aspect of self-acceptance. However, it deserves a deeper examination in the context of healing and transformation. Many Starseeds, due to their heightened intuition and empathy, may carry a heavier burden of self-criticism. They may hold themselves to impossibly high standards, judging themselves harshly for perceived flaws or past mistakes. This self-judgment prevents them from moving forward and embracing their full potential. Self-forgiveness, therefore, is not simply about acknowledging past errors; it's about releasing the self-criticism, accepting imperfection, and embracing the process of growth and evolution.

A powerful technique for practicing self-forgiveness involves a **structured process of reflection and release.** Begin by identifying the specific event or situation that causes you self-reproach. Write down all the thoughts and feelings associated with it. Don't censor yourself; let the emotions flow freely onto the page. Once you've fully expressed your feelings, try to understand the situation from a more compassionate perspective. Ask yourself: what was I learning at that time? What were my intentions? What could I have done differently, given my level of understanding at the time?

Acknowledge your past self with kindness and understanding, recognizing that you acted within the context of your own limitations.

Visualizing the release of the negative energy associated with the event can be a profoundly effective tool. Imagine the pain, guilt, or shame manifested as a physical object—a heavy stone, a dark cloud, or any symbol that resonates with you. Visualize yourself placing this object on a raft, watching it float away down a river, carrying your burden with it. As the object drifts farther and farther away, visualize a feeling of lightness and peace filling your being. This visualization technique allows for a symbolic letting go of the past and a conscious step toward emotional freedom.

Forgiving others presents a different, yet equally crucial, challenge.

Holding onto resentment towards others creates a significant energetic blockage, preventing us from moving forward and experiencing true freedom. It's important to understand that forgiveness isn't condoning the actions of others. It's not about excusing harmful behaviors; it's about releasing the grip of negativity that those actions have on you. It's about reclaiming your own emotional power and freeing yourself from the chains of bitterness.

Forgiving others doesn't necessarily mean reconciliation or re-establishing contact. Sometimes, the healthiest path is simply to release the negative energy associated with the person and the situation. The process of forgiving others often mirrors that of self-forgiveness: acknowledging the hurt, expressing your emotions, and then consciously choosing to release the burden of resentment. Write a letter to the person, expressing your hurt and anger without sending it. This can be a cathartic way to release pent-up emotions without necessarily confronting the other person. Then, symbolically release the letter, perhaps burning it or burying it.

Meditation plays a vital role in both self-forgiveness and forgiving others. Mindful meditation allows us to access a space of inner peace and calm where we can observe our emotions without judgment. Through focused breathing and attention to the present moment, we can detach from the emotional grip of resentment and anger. Guided meditations specifically designed for forgiveness can be particularly helpful, guiding you through the process of releasing negative energy and cultivating compassion. Even simple deep breathing exercises can help calm the nervous system, creating space for more balanced emotional processing.

Energy healing techniques, such as Reiki or energy clearing, can also support the process of forgiveness. These techniques help to clear energetic blockages caused by resentment and anger, restoring a sense of balance and harmony within your energy field. Many Starseeds are naturally attuned to energy work, finding that these practices amplify their healing and transformation. Working with an experienced energy healer can be beneficial, providing guidance and support during this process.

The transformative power of forgiveness extends far beyond personal emotional healing. It unlocks spiritual growth by allowing us to connect more deeply with our higher selves and the universal energy that flows through us all. When we release the weight of unforgiveness, we create space for love, compassion, and joy to enter our lives. We become more open to receiving the abundance and blessings the universe has in store for us. For Starseeds, this spiritual connection is especially vital, enabling them to access their higher purpose and fulfill their unique mission on Earth.

Remember, the journey of forgiveness takes time, patience, and self-compassion. There will be moments when the pain resurfaces, when the urge to hold onto resentment is strong. But with each act of forgiveness, with each release of negativity, you are consciously choosing a path of healing and transformation. You are freeing yourself from the past and stepping into a brighter, more empowered future. Embrace the process, and trust in the transformative power of forgiveness to guide you towards a life of greater peace, joy, and spiritual fulfillment. Your journey as a Starseed is one of evolution and ascension, and forgiveness is a vital key to unlocking your full potential. Embrace this journey with courage and grace, and know that you are never alone. The universe supports you every step of the way. Let the journey of self-acceptance and forgiveness lead you to the highest expression of your magnificent Starseed self.

SPIRITUAL TRANSCENDENCE
Through Suffering

Suffering, in its myriad forms, is an inescapable aspect of the human experience. While we naturally recoil from pain, hardship, and loss, a closer examination reveals a profound paradox: suffering can serve as a crucible for spiritual transcendence. This is not to romanticize pain, but rather to explore the transformative potential inherent within even the most agonizing experiences. The path to spiritual growth, particularly for those with heightened sensitivities like Starseeds, often involves navigating significant challenges. It is through these trials that we can develop resilience, deepen our understanding of ourselves and the universe, and ultimately, discover a greater sense of purpose.

Many spiritual traditions offer perspectives on the meaning and purpose of suffering. Buddhism, for instance, views suffering (dukkha) as an inherent part of existence, stemming from attachment and craving. The path to liberation, or Nirvana, involves cultivating wisdom and compassion to overcome these attachments.

Christianity, similarly, often frames suffering as a pathway to spiritual growth, drawing parallels between Christ's sacrifice and the transformative power of personal hardship. The concept of "carrying one's cross" reflects the idea that challenges can refine the soul and deepen faith. Other traditions, such as certain schools of Hinduism, emphasize the cyclical nature of life, death, and rebirth, with suffering serving as a catalyst for karmic evolution. The soul, through experiencing various forms of suffering, gradually sheds its imperfections and progresses towards enlightenment.

From a psychological perspective, suffering can act as a catalyst for personal growth and resilience. When faced with adversity, we are forced to confront our limitations and develop coping mechanisms.

Post-traumatic growth, a well-documented phenomenon, demonstrates that individuals can emerge from traumatic experiences with enhanced self-awareness, increased empathy, and a renewed sense of meaning and purpose.

The very process of struggling to overcome adversity builds emotional strength and resilience, equipping us to navigate future challenges with greater ease and composure.

For Starseeds, with their often amplified sensitivity, the intensity of suffering can be particularly profound. They may feel the emotional weight of the world more keenly, experiencing pain and empathy with greater depth than many others. This heightened sensitivity, while sometimes overwhelming, can also be a gift. Their heightened awareness allows for a deeper understanding of the human condition and a more profound connection to the interconnectedness of all beings. The very intensity of their suffering can drive them towards a deeper exploration of spiritual truth and a relentless search for meaning.

This deeper understanding is not readily achieved through comfortable circumstances. ***The struggle to find meaning in the face of suffering can lead to a richer, more authentic spiritual experience.*** For Starseeds, this heightened awareness and intensified connection to the universe can enable them to draw upon universal energy for support and guidance. This inward journey can lead to a profound spiritual awakening.

However, recognizing the potential for spiritual growth within suffering is not about passively accepting hardship. It's not about enduring pain without striving for healing or change. Instead, it involves approaching suffering with mindful awareness and actively seeking to extract lessons and wisdom from difficult experiences. This involves cultivating self-compassion, allowing ourselves to feel the pain without judgment or self-recrimination, and acknowledging that our experiences are part of a larger cosmic plan.

Several practices can facilitate this process of finding meaning and purpose in suffering. Mindfulness meditation, for instance, can help us to observe our thoughts and emotions without judgment, creating space to process our experiences without being overwhelmed. Journaling can also be a powerful tool, enabling us to articulate our feelings, reflect on our challenges, and identify potential pathways towards growth. Engaging in creative expression, through art, music, or writing, can provide an outlet for emotions and facilitate a deeper understanding of our inner landscape.

Connecting with nature can also be profoundly healing. Spending time outdoors, surrounded by the natural world, can provide a sense of grounding and perspective, reminding us of the enduring strength and resilience of life itself. Engaging with supportive communities, whether online or in person, can provide a sense of belonging and shared experience, offering comfort and encouragement during challenging times. Sharing our experiences and listening to the stories of others can remind us that we are not alone in our struggles.

Engaging in acts of service and compassion can be profoundly transformative. When we focus on giving to others, our perspective shifts from our own suffering towards the needs of others. ***This act of selfless giving can create a sense of purpose and meaning, diminishing the intensity of our personal pain and fostering a deeper connection to our spiritual essence.*** For Starseeds, whose heightened empathy often motivates them towards altruistic actions, engaging in compassionate service can be particularly powerful in fostering healing and transformation.

The path of spiritual transcendence through suffering is a deeply personal one. There is no single "right" way to navigate hardship.

What is essential is a willingness to embrace the challenges, to cultivate self-compassion, and to actively seek meaning and purpose within the experience. It is through these trials, through the refining fire of adversity, that we can unlock our deepest potential for growth, spiritual awareness, and a more profound connection to the universe and our place within it.

This journey, while often painful, ultimately leads to a richer, more authentic, and fulfilling life, empowering us to embrace the full spectrum of the human experience with grace and resilience. The journey of a Starseed, with its heightened sensitivity and connection to the cosmic realm, is evidence to the power of transformation that can arise from the embrace of even the most intense forms of suffering.

The ability to transform suffering into spiritual growth is a hallmark of the Starseed journey, a legacy to their resilience, inner strength, and profound connection to the universe. This process is not simply about overcoming challenges; it's about integrating them into the very fabric of one's being, emerging stronger, wiser, and more deeply connected to oneself and the cosmos.

The resulting transformation transcends the limitations of the individual experience, becoming a source of inspiration and guidance for others on their own paths of spiritual evolution. The journey is one of constant growth and transformation, guided by the unwavering support of the universe and the inner strength of the Starseed soul.

Embrace the lessons, embrace the challenges, and allow the suffering to become the catalyst for your own unique and magnificent ascension.

UNDERSTANDING
Indigo Children

The exploration of Starseeds and their profound connection to universal energy naturally leads us to consider a closely related concept: Indigo Children. While not all Indigo Children are considered Starseeds, and not all Starseeds identify as Indigo Children, there's a significant overlap in their characteristics and the experiences they often share. Understanding the unique attributes of Indigo Children illuminates another facet of this broader tapestry of heightened sensitivity and spiritual awakening.

The term "Indigo Child" emerged in the late 20th century within the New Age movement, describing Children born after the 1970s who were perceived as possessing unusual qualities and spiritual gifts. Unlike previous generations, these Children were often described as exhibiting a heightened level of intuition, empathy, and creativity, along with a strong sense of independence and a deep connection to nature. Their sensitivity extended beyond the emotional; many demonstrated a heightened awareness of subtle energies and a profound understanding of interconnectedness. These characteristics weren't simply quirks; they were perceived as integral aspects of their being, representing a new wave of consciousness unfolding upon the planet.

The core characteristics attributed to Indigo Children often include an intense sensitivity to their environment. This isn't merely emotional sensitivity, but also a sensitivity to electromagnetic fields, noise pollution, and the emotional states of those around them. This can manifest as an aversion to crowds, loud noises, or strong artificial lights. In some cases, it leads to sensory overload and an increased susceptibility to anxiety or emotional overwhelm.

However, this sensitivity is also a conduit for profound empathy and intuition. Indigo Children often possess an exceptional ability to understand the feelings and intentions of others, sometimes even before those feelings are consciously articulated. Their heightened intuition can manifest in various ways, from uncanny hunches to precognitive dreams.

Creativity is another hallmark of the Indigo Child experience. They often demonstrate exceptional artistic talent, innovative thinking, and a capacity for unconventional problem-solving. This isn't limited to conventional artistic expressions; it extends to imaginative play, unconventional thinking styles, and a natural inclination towards questioning established norms and paradigms. This innate creativity often serves as a powerful tool for self-expression and personal growth, allowing them to navigate the complexities of life with a unique perspective.

Furthermore, Indigo Children often exhibit a strong sense of independence and self-reliance. They are not easily swayed by external pressures and possess a clear understanding of their own values and beliefs. This independence is not necessarily rebellious, but rather a reflection of their innate self-awareness and a deep understanding of their individual path. This inner strength allows them to navigate societal expectations with grace and determination.

However, this combination of heightened sensitivity, exceptional creativity, and unwavering independence can also pose challenges.

The intense awareness of their surroundings can make them vulnerable to negativity, causing emotional exhaustion or feelings of being overwhelmed. The unconventional thinking often leads to misunderstandings with those who adhere to more conventional viewpoints. *The intense need for authenticity and self-expression can sometimes lead to conflict with traditional educational systems and societal norms. It's crucial to remember that the Indigo Child experience isn't simply a set of convenient labels; it represents a complex interplay of individual traits and societal interactions.*

Historically, the concept of Indigo Children has become intertwined with other New Age ideologies, particularly the concept of Starseeds. Some believe that Indigo Children represent a new generation of souls incarnating on Earth, carrying advanced spiritual knowledge and unique abilities to assist in the planet's evolution. These souls, some propose, are not solely of Earthly origin but possess an extraterrestrial connection, echoing the Starseed belief system.

The relationship between Indigo Children and Starseeds isn't entirely clear-cut; there's significant overlap but also distinctions. While many who identify as Starseeds exhibit characteristics aligned with Indigo Children, not all Indigo Children perceive themselves as Starseeds. The core difference lies in the explicit belief in a non-terrestrial origin. Starseeds are consciously aware of a spiritual connection to a celestial body or realm beyond Earth, often accompanied by memories or dreams hinting at a past life in another dimension. Indigo Children, while possessing unique spiritual gifts, might not necessarily identify with the Starseed narrative. They might focus on their earthly mission and spiritual growth without explicitly connecting it to a non-terrestrial background.

However, both groups share many common threads. Their heightened sensitivity, innate intuition, and profound creative abilities are often observed in both. Both Indigo Children and Starseeds frequently exhibit a deep yearning for purpose and a strong desire to contribute positively to the world. They often display a heightened sense of compassion and a deep concern for environmental and social justice issues. This shared drive for positive change underscores a deep-seated connection to something larger than themselves, a connection often described as a sense of being part of a greater cosmic plan.

In essence, the Indigo Child experience can be seen as a specific manifestation of the broader Starseed phenomenon. *Indigo Children represent a subset of Starseeds, sharing many of the same traits but without the conscious awareness of a non-terrestrial origin.* Both share a crucial role in the evolutionary process of humanity and the planet. Their heightened intuition, potent creativity, and unparalleled empathy represent valuable assets in navigating the complexities of the modern world and creating a more compassionate and sustainable future. It is through understanding and embracing these unique individuals that we can further unlock the potential for spiritual growth and collective evolution.

The challenges faced by Indigo Children, much like those encountered by Starseeds, often stem from a mismatch between their heightened sensitivity and the expectations of a society that might not fully understand their unique perspective. The intensity of their emotions, the unconventional nature of their thoughts, and the depth of their empathy can lead to feelings of isolation and alienation. This underscores the importance of fostering supportive communities where these individuals can find acceptance, understanding, and a sense of belonging. Providing appropriate support systems that acknowledge and validate their unique experiences is crucial for their emotional well-being and spiritual growth.

Additionally, understanding the role of suffering in the lives of Indigo Children is critical. Just like Starseeds, they may experience the pain of the world more deeply, often carrying the emotional burden of those around them. This heightened sensitivity, while potentially overwhelming, can also serve as a catalyst for profound compassion and a deep desire to alleviate suffering. Navigating this intense emotional landscape requires self-compassion, self-awareness, and the cultivation of healthy coping mechanisms.

Recognizing the unique gifts of Indigo Children and their potential contribution to a more conscious and compassionate world is essential. ***Their presence represents a shift in consciousness, a movement towards greater empathy, intuition, and creative problem-solving.*** By fostering understanding and acceptance, we create space for their unique abilities to flourish, enabling them to realize their full potential and contribute positively to the evolution of humanity and the planet. Their journey, much like that of Starseeds, is one of ongoing growth, transformation, and the gradual integration of their extraordinary abilities into the fabric of their lives and the world around them. Embracing their unique gifts is not merely an act of compassion; it's a crucial step towards creating a more conscious and harmonious future for all.

The journey of both Indigo Children and Starseeds underscores the interconnectedness of all beings and the profound potential for spiritual growth and transformation when we embrace the full spectrum of human—and perhaps extra-terrestrial—experience.

Indigo Children *and* Universal Energy

The exploration of Indigo Children and their inherent connection to universal energy unveils a profound and often misunderstood aspect of their unique gifts. Unlike the more widely recognized aspects of their heightened sensitivity and creativity, their interaction with universal energy lies at the heart of their transformative potential.

This interaction is not simply a passive reception; it's a dynamic interplay, a constant exchange and flow of energy that shapes their experiences and empowers their unique contributions to the world.

Indigo Children, with their inherently heightened sensory perception, often experience universal energy in ways that many others cannot. The subtle vibrations, the unseen currents of energy that flow through all things— these are not abstract concepts for them but tangible realities. They feel the pulse of the planet, the ebb and flow of cosmic energies, and the energetic signatures of individuals and environments. This heightened awareness isn't always comfortable; it can lead to sensory overload, emotional overwhelm, and a deep sensitivity to environmental imbalances. However, this same sensitivity is the key to unlocking their extraordinary potential.

Their ability to perceive and interact with universal energy is not limited to passive observation. *Many Indigo Children possess an innate capacity to channel and manipulate these energies for healing, creativity, and personal transformation.* This isn't necessarily a conscious or deliberate act; it often manifests spontaneously through their artistic expressions, their empathetic connections with others, and their innate ability to sense and respond to the needs of the environment. For instance, an Indigo Child might find themselves inexplicably drawn to a specific location in nature, a place imbued with potent healing energies. They might intuitively understand the emotional state of another person, subtly shifting the energetic field to promote harmony and balance. Their creative work might become a conduit for universal energy, channeling inspiration and transforming emotions into powerful forms of self-expression.

The Indigo Children – not merely Children, but **heralds**. They feel the electric vibration in the air, a palpable shift in the planetary energy field, a resonance deep in their bones. These aren't simply kids with heightened empathy; they are conduits, vessels crackling with a power both ancient and startlingly new. Their eyes, pools of molten amethyst, reflect a universe unseen by the rest of us – a universe pulsing with a symphony of interconnectedness, a noise of suffering and potential. Their intuition isn't a whisper; it's a roar, a visceral knowing that tears through the fabric of illusion, exposing the raw, bleeding heart of reality. They taste the bitterness of injustice, smell the decay of a dying world, and feel the phantom limb of a future yet unborn, a future they are fiercely determined to sculpt. Some fear their intensity, their unyielding gaze piercing through societal masks, stripping away the veneer of normalcy to reveal the stark truth. Others are drawn to their incandescent flame, a lighthouse promising a world reborn. These are not mere catalysts for change; they are the **change** itself. Their empathy is a powerful wave, threatening to drown the apathy that suffocates our planet. Their connection to the universal energy field isn't some airy-fairy notion; it's a tangible force, a fresh power that could either heal or shatter our world. They stand at the precipice of a new era, a generation poised to rewrite the rules of human existence, forging a future shaped in compassion, or consumed by the fires of their own untamed potential. The choice, it seems, rests not in their hands, but in ours.

Indigo Children are not merely intuitive; they are seismic tremors in the placid pond of normalcy. Their minds, electric storms crackling with unconventional thought, shatter the brittle glass of established order. The friction ignites conflict, a rare, burning fire that scorches the comfortable complacency of the status quo. Yet from these ashes, phoenix-like, rise innovative solutions, perspectives so radical that inspire for a mind revolution. Justice isn't a concept for them; it's a visceral need, a thrumming pulse felt in the very marrow of their bones.

Compassion isn't a virtue; it's a way of life, sweeping away indifference with its unrelenting force. Their responsibility to the Earth, to the ravaged global community, is a sacred oath, whispered on the wind, etched in starlight. This interconnectedness isn't some airy-fairy notion; it's a tangible presence, a web of pure energy vibrating beneath their skin, a symphony of life pulsating with a power that both terrifies and exhilarates. They feel the planet's wounds as their own, the cries of suffering echoing in their very souls, a painful, haunting melody only they can truly hear. Their burden is immense, a weight of understanding that would crush lesser beings, yet it fuels them, drives them, shaping them into something both magnificent and terrifying.

Understanding the energetic signatures of Indigo Children is not merely an intellectual exercise; it is a crucial step in acknowledging the evolving energetic landscape of our planet. Their heightened spiritual awareness and intuitive abilities are not anomalies; they are reflections of the expanding consciousness of humanity. Their presence challenges us to re-evaluate our worldviews, question existing structures, and embrace a future where intuition, empathy, and interconnectedness are central to the human experience.

The role of Indigo Children in shifting global consciousness is profound and potentially transformative.

Their heightened sensitivity allows them to perceive the energetic imbalances that plague our world—the discord, the negativity, and the disharmony that permeate our collective consciousness. Their innate empathy fuels a deep desire to heal these imbalances and create a more harmonious and sustainable world. This is not just a theoretical concept; their actions often reflect this inherent desire. They might be deeply involved in environmental activism, advocating for social justice, or pursuing creative endeavors that promote understanding and compassion. Their very presence acts as a catalyst for change, inspiring others to embrace a more conscious and responsible way of living.

Harnessing their unique energy signatures is a critical aspect of personal growth and empowerment for Indigo Children. This involves understanding the nature of their sensitivity and developing healthy coping mechanisms to manage sensory overload and emotional overwhelm. Practices like meditation, grounding techniques, and spending time in nature can significantly aid in this process. Meditation allows them to connect with their inner selves and to regulate the flow of universal energy through their bodies.

Grounding techniques help them to anchor their energy to the earth, providing stability and reducing feelings of being overwhelmed. Spending time in nature allows them to immerse themselves in the healing energies of the natural world, restoring balance and promoting emotional well-being.

The challenges faced by Indigo Children in navigating their relationship with universal energy are significant. ***The intensity of their energetic sensitivity can make them highly susceptible to negativity and emotional exhaustion. They often absorb the emotional burdens of others, leaving them feeling drained and overwhelmed. This vulnerability underscores the importance of developing strong boundaries and learning to protect their energy from external influences.*** This might involve consciously choosing their environments, limiting exposure to negativity, and practicing techniques to shield themselves from energetic intrusions.

Understanding their unique energy signatures is crucial for self-acceptance and self-compassion. Indigo Children often feel different from their peers, leading to feelings of isolation and alienation. Recognizing and embracing their unique gifts, their heightened sensitivity, and their potent connection to universal energy is a critical step towards self-acceptance and self-love. This understanding allows them to see their differences not as weaknesses but as strengths, empowering them to embrace their unique path and to make their unique contribution to the world.

The process of self-discovery for Indigo Children often involves exploring various practices and modalities that resonate with their energy signatures. This might involve energy healing, sound therapy, crystal healing, or other practices designed to work with subtle energies. These practices can help them to understand their energy patterns, to clear energetic blockages, and to enhance their connection with universal energy. However, it's crucial to find practices that feel authentic and resonate deeply with their individual needs and experiences.

The journey of an Indigo Child is one of constant learning, growth, and self-discovery. It's a path that requires courage, resilience, and a deep commitment to self-awareness. Their heightened sensitivity can be a source of both profound joy and significant challenges. Navigating this spectrum of experiences requires self-compassion, a strong support system, and a commitment to fostering healthy coping mechanisms.

The connection between Indigo Children and universal energy is a proof of the profound interconnectedness of all beings. Their unique gifts are not merely individual attributes; they are expressions of a larger cosmic force, a universal intelligence that seeks to manifest itself through them. By understanding and embracing their unique energy signatures, Indigo Children unlock their full potential, not just for themselves, but for the entire planet. Their journey is a reminder that we are all interconnected, that our individual experiences are interwoven with the fabric of universal energy, and that every contribution, however small, can have a profound impact on the collective consciousness.

Their journey is a confirmation of the transformative power of embracing our unique gifts and utilizing our connection to the universal energy for the betterment of ourselves and the world. This is not simply a New Age concept; it's a profound truth that is reflected in the lives and experiences of these remarkable individuals. The path of an Indigo Child, therefore, is a journey of empowerment, of realizing one's full potential, and of contributing to a world that embraces diversity, compassion, and the transformative power of universal energy. It is a journey that deserves our understanding, support, and unwavering respect.

Their emergence marks a pivotal moment in human history, a time of profound transformation and a bold step towards a future defined by greater consciousness, compassion, and a renewed sense of interconnectedness. ***Their path is not merely personal; it is a collective journey, one that invites us all to embrace our own unique energetic signatures and contribute to the creation of a more enlightened and harmonious world.*** Their lives offer us valuable lessons in embracing our own intuition, cultivating compassion, and stepping into our roles as conscious creators of a better future. Their experiences highlight the profound influence of energy on individual lives and the critical role of energetic understanding in navigating the complexities of modern life and shaping a more conscious future. It is a future where the energies of compassion, understanding, and interconnectedness are at the forefront of human interaction and progress.

The evolution of consciousness is not a passive process; it is an active participation in shaping our individual and collective realities.

Challenges *and* Gifts *of* Indigo Children

The journey of an Indigo Child is not without its trials. Their heightened sensitivity, while a source of profound insight and creativity, can also be a significant source of challenge. The world, often designed for those with less intense perceptions, can feel overwhelming, jarring, even hostile. This dissonance between their inner world and the external reality often leads to feelings of being misunderstood, different, and alone. They may struggle to articulate their experiences, leading to frustration and isolation. The intensity of their emotions, amplified by their heightened sensory perception, can manifest as emotional volatility, making it difficult to navigate social situations and maintain healthy relationships.

One of the most significant challenges Indigo Children face is the overwhelming influx of sensory information. The world bombards them with stimuli—sounds, sights, smells, and energies—that many others filter out unconsciously. This constant sensory barrage can lead to sensory overload, manifesting as anxiety, irritability, and even physical symptoms like headaches or digestive issues. Imagine the experience of hearing every conversation in a crowded room simultaneously, or feeling the emotional weight of every person present. For an Indigo Child, this is not just a metaphor; it's their lived reality. This necessitates the development of coping mechanisms, learning to selectively filter sensory input and manage the intensity of their experiences.

Furthermore, their profound empathy often becomes a double-edged sword. Their ability to deeply connect with the emotions of others is a beautiful gift, allowing them to provide profound comfort and understanding. However, this empathy can also lead to emotional exhaustion, as they absorb the emotional burdens of those around them. They might feel the pain of others as keenly as their own, leaving them drained and overwhelmed. Learning to set healthy boundaries is crucial for their well-being, allowing them to connect with others compassionately without sacrificing their own emotional equilibrium. This might involve consciously limiting exposure to intense emotional situations, developing techniques to shield themselves energetically, or simply prioritizing time alone to recharge and process their experiences.

Another significant hurdle Indigo Children often face is a lack of understanding from those around them. Their unconventional thinking, their intense emotional responses, and their often unconventional methods of expressing themselves can lead to misunderstanding and even judgment. This can manifest as a feeling of being labeled as "difficult," "sensitive," or even "weird." The lack of support and validation can fuel feelings of isolation, self-doubt, and low self-esteem. It's crucial for adults, particularly parents and educators, to create a supportive and validating environment where Indigo Children feel safe to express themselves authentically.

Understanding their unique needs, validating their experiences, and fostering their sense of self-worth are essential aspects of helping them thrive.

Despite these challenges, the gifts of Indigo Children are profound and transformative. Their heightened sensitivity isn't just a source of difficulty; it's the very foundation of their unique abilities. Their enhanced perception allows them to see beyond the surface, to grasp the underlying patterns and interconnectedness of things. This leads to innovative thinking, creative problem-solving, and an intuitive understanding of complex systems. They are often gifted artists, musicians, writers, or inventors, expressing their inner world through various creative outlets. Their creations frequently reflect a deep understanding of human emotion, universal truths, and the intricate workings of the universe.

Moreover, Indigo Children possess a natural inclination towards empathy and compassion. Their ability to deeply feel the emotions of others fuels a strong desire to heal and improve the world. They may be drawn to careers in fields such as healthcare, education, social work, or environmental activism. Their inherent drive to create a more compassionate and harmonious world makes them powerful agents of positive change. They possess a natural ability to sense energetic imbalances and intuitively understand the needs of others, leading them to act as catalysts for transformation in their communities and beyond.

Their connection to the universal energy provides them with a unique perspective, allowing them to perceive the interconnectedness of all things and to intuitively understand the underlying patterns of the universe. This understanding transcends the limitations of the physical world, offering them insight into universal laws, energetic flows, and the profound interconnectedness of all life. This intuitive grasp of energetic principles often allows them to manifest their intentions with ease, attracting opportunities and resources that align with their unique purpose.

Nurturing and supporting Indigo Children requires a deep understanding of their unique needs and challenges. Creating a safe and supportive environment where they feel understood and validated is paramount. This involves fostering open communication, actively listening to their experiences, and validating their emotions, even if they seem intense or unconventional. Parents, educators, and other caregivers should strive to create an environment that celebrates their individuality and encourages their unique talents and abilities. This may require patience, understanding, and a willingness to adapt traditional methods to meet their specific needs.

Practical strategies for supporting Indigo Children include providing opportunities for creative expression, such as art therapy, music therapy, or drama. Encouraging them to spend time in nature, where they can ground their energy and connect with the earth's healing vibrations, is also beneficial. Introducing practices such as meditation, mindfulness, and yoga can help them to manage their heightened sensitivity and regulate their emotional responses. These practices can help them to develop their innate abilities and to cultivate inner peace and balance.

It is equally vital to encourage self-care practices and provide tools for self-regulation.

Teaching them effective coping mechanisms for managing sensory overload and emotional intensity is essential.

This might include techniques such as deep breathing exercises, grounding techniques, and sensory regulation strategies. It is crucial to create a supportive environment where they feel safe to express their needs and to seek help when needed. Encouraging them to build a strong support network of friends, family, and mentors who understand and accept them is also essential for their overall well-being. These support systems can provide them with the emotional validation and practical assistance they need to navigate their unique journey.

The journey of an Indigo Child is one of constant growth, learning, and self-discovery. It is a path that demands resilience, self-compassion, and an unwavering commitment to understanding their unique gifts. While the challenges they face can be significant, their unique talents and abilities hold immense potential for positive change in the world. By fostering a supportive environment and providing the appropriate tools and resources, we can empower Indigo Children to embrace their gifts, overcome their challenges, and make a meaningful contribution to a world that desperately needs their compassion, creativity, and profound understanding.

Their path, though sometimes arduous, is ultimately a path of profound empowerment, a testament to the transformative power of embracing one's unique gifts and using them to create a brighter future for all. This is not just about understanding a specific group of individuals; it is about understanding the potential within all of us to connect with the universal energy and use that connection for the betterment of ourselves and the world.

THE SYNERGISTIC RELATIONSHIP
Between Starseeds *and* Indigo Children

The journey of the Indigo Child, as we've explored, is one of heightened sensitivity and profound empathy, often accompanied by a unique perspective on the world and an innate drive for positive change. But what happens when this potent energy intersects with the path of a Starseed? This is where the potential for a truly synergistic relationship emerges, a powerful collaboration that amplifies the individual gifts of each and creates a transformative force for the greater good.

As we previously analyzed, Starseeds, often described as souls originating from other planetary systems or dimensions, carry within them a distinct cosmic consciousness. Their experiences may include vivid dreams, a strong sense of otherness, and a profound longing for something beyond the confines of this earthly realm. They frequently possess a deep understanding of universal principles and an intuitive grasp of energetic dynamics that often surpasses the understanding of their contemporaries. This inherent connection to the cosmos equips them with a unique perspective, a heightened awareness of the interconnectedness of all things, and a profound understanding of the universe's intricate workings.

The intersection of the Indigo Child's heightened empathy and the Starseed's cosmic consciousness creates a potent combination. The Indigo Child's sensitivity acts as a powerful amplifier, allowing the Starseed's subtle energetic insights to manifest more readily in the physical world. The Indigo Child's inherent drive for positive change finds purpose and direction through the Starseed's broader cosmic vision. Imagine an Indigo Child, intensely compassionate and driven to help others, working alongside a Starseed who possesses an innate understanding of universal healing modalities. Together, they could form a dynamic force for healing and transformation, impacting countless lives through their collaborative efforts.

This synergy is not limited to altruistic endeavors. The creative potential unleashed by this collaboration can be profound. The Indigo Child's creative expression, often vibrant and emotionally charged, finds a new dimension when infused with the Starseed's cosmic perspective. The Starseed's deep connection to universal patterns and archetypes provides a framework for the Indigo Child's creativity, guiding it toward innovative solutions and groundbreaking creations. A Starseed musician, for instance, may possess an intuitive understanding of sound frequencies and their impact on consciousness. Collaborating with an Indigo Child composer, deeply empathetic and attuned to human emotion, could lead to music that heals, inspires, and elevates consciousness on a global scale.

Consider the example of a Starseed scientist, whose innate understanding of universal principles guides their research towards uncovering new technologies or healing modalities. Their collaboration with an Indigo Child researcher, deeply empathic and attuned to the needs of others, ensures that these discoveries are implemented ethically and responsibly, benefiting humanity as a whole. This synergy is not simply additive; it's exponential. The combined potential of these two energy types far surpasses the sum of their individual contributions.

However, this synergistic relationship is not without its challenges. The heightened sensitivities of both Indigo Children and Starseeds can create points of friction. The overwhelming sensory input experienced by Indigo Children might be amplified by the Starseed's cosmic awareness, leading to periods of intense emotional or energetic overload. This necessitates a deep understanding of each other's needs and a willingness to develop effective coping mechanisms for managing this intensity.

Open communication, mutual respect, and a shared understanding of their individual and collective goals are paramount for the success of this partnership. This requires patience, self-awareness, and a willingness to adapt and compromise. Learning to create boundaries, both individually and collectively, is crucial for maintaining emotional and energetic balance. Practicing grounding techniques, meditation, and other mindfulness practices can help to mitigate the intensity of their experiences and foster a deeper sense of inner peace.

The path of both Indigo Children and Starseeds is often marked by periods of isolation and misunderstanding. Their unique perspectives and heightened sensitivity can make it challenging to connect with those who lack a similar understanding. Their collaborative relationship, however, provides a powerful antidote to this isolation. By finding each other, they discover a sense of belonging, a shared purpose, and a mutual understanding that allows them to navigate the complexities of their journey with greater ease and resilience. They become each other's anchor, a source of strength, support, and unconditional acceptance.

Examples of this synergy can be found throughout history and in contemporary society. Many artists, musicians, writers, and inventors who have profoundly impacted humanity may have been unwitting collaborators between these two energetic types. Their visionary creations, often characterized by a profound understanding of human emotion and universal principles, may reflect the combined influence of Starseed intuition and Indigo Child empathy. Their capacity to break boundaries, challenge norms, and envision a better future reflects the power of this synergistic relationship.

The synergistic relationship between Starseeds and Indigo Children extends beyond the realm of individual achievements. It encompasses a collective mission, a shared purpose that transcends personal aspirations. They often find themselves drawn to collaborative endeavors that benefit humanity as a whole, such as environmental activism, social justice initiatives, or the development of sustainable technologies. Their combined energy and vision become a powerful catalyst for positive change, inspiring and motivating others to join their cause.

The study of this unique connection is still in its nascent stages. There are no standardized tests or scientific methodologies to definitively identify Starseeds or to empirically measure the synergistic effects of their interactions with Indigo Children.

However, the subjective evidence and personal testimonies of individuals who identify with these energy types are compelling and strongly suggest a powerful and transformative dynamic at play. It's a proof of the interconnectedness of all things, a reflection of the universal energy that flows through us all.

The relationship between Starseeds and Indigo Children is not merely a concept or a theory. It's a living, breathing reality, manifesting in countless interactions and collaborations that are reshaping our world. It's a potent reminder that our individual gifts, when combined with a deep understanding of ourselves and others, can create a force for positive change that transcends limitations and inspires a brighter future for all. It's a call to embrace our unique abilities, to connect with the universal energy that flows through us, and to work together to create a world that reflects the profound beauty and interconnectedness of all life. The future, it seems, belongs to those who embrace their cosmic inheritance and use it to create a world where compassion, creativity, and cosmic awareness thrive. Their journey is a journey of collaboration, a harmonious union of souls working together to weave a legacy of light, healing, and transformative change. This is not merely a spiritual belief; it's a potent energy field brimming with potential, waiting to be realized.

SUPPORTING
Indigo Children's Growth *and* Development

Supporting the unique needs of an Indigo Child requires a multifaceted approach that goes beyond traditional methods. Their heightened sensitivity, coupled with their often intense emotional landscape, demands a nurturing environment that fosters self-expression, emotional regulation, and a deep sense of self-acceptance. This journey isn't about "fixing" the Child, but rather about empowering them to navigate their extraordinary gifts with grace and resilience.

FOR PARENTS, the journey begins with self-reflection. Understanding your own emotional responses and patterns is crucial. Indigo Children are highly perceptive, often mirroring the emotional climate of their environment. If you are constantly stressed or anxious, your Child will likely pick up on this, potentially amplifying their own sensitivities. Prioritizing self-care – through meditation, yoga, spending time in nature, or engaging in creative pursuits – is not a luxury but a necessity. Your emotional well-being directly impacts your ability to support your Child's growth.

OPEN COMMUNICATION is paramount. Create a safe space where your Child feels comfortable expressing their emotions, no matter how intense or unusual. Active listening, rather than judgment or dismissal, is key. Validate their feelings, even if you don't fully understand them. Phrases like, "I hear you're feeling overwhelmed," or "That sounds really frustrating," can go a long way in creating a sense of connection and understanding. Avoid dismissing their experiences with comments like, "You're too sensitive," or "Just get over it." These diminish their feelings and undermine their trust.

ENCOURAGE SELF-EXPRESSION through creative outlets. Art, music, dance, writing – these are powerful tools for Indigo Children to process their emotions and connect with their inner world. Don't pressure them into conforming to traditional expectations or activities. Let them explore their passions freely, even if they seem unconventional. Their creativity is not just a hobby; it's a vital aspect of their self-expression and emotional regulation.

UNDERSTANDING THEIR SENSORY SENSITIVITIES is vital. Indigo Children are often hypersensitive to light, sound, textures, and smells. Create a calming environment that minimizes overwhelming sensory input. This might involve using soft lighting, playing calming music, or minimizing clutter. Be mindful of the types of clothing and fabrics your Child wears, ensuring they are comfortable and don't cause irritation. Sensory integration therapy can be incredibly beneficial in helping Indigo Children process sensory input more effectively.

ACADEMICALLY, Indigo Children often excel in certain areas while struggling in others. They may be highly intuitive and creative but may find traditional schooling methods restrictive or frustrating. Collaboration with educators is key. Educators need to understand the Child's unique learning style and adapt their teaching methods accordingly. Project-based learning, independent study, and alternative schooling options may be more suitable than traditional classroom environments.

In terms of social interactions, Indigo Children may struggle with navigating social dynamics. Their intense empathy can make them vulnerable to the emotional energies of others. They may withdraw from social situations or become overwhelmed by social interactions. Encourage social skills development through activities that allow them to connect with others in comfortable, low-pressure settings. Small group interactions, extracurricular activities that align with their interests, or even one-on-one friendships, can all be beneficial. Teaching them about emotional boundaries and healthy communication skills is also crucial.

Beyond parental support, fostering a supportive community is crucial. Connecting with other parents of Indigo Children can provide invaluable support and understanding. Sharing experiences, strategies, and resources can make a significant difference. Support groups, online forums, and workshops specifically designed for parents of Indigo Children provide a safe space to connect and learn from one another.

FOR EDUCATORS, recognizing and supporting Indigo Children in the classroom requires a shift in perspective. Traditional teaching methods may not be effective for these highly sensitive and intuitive learners. Embrace differentiated instruction, allowing students to learn at their own pace and in ways that suit their unique learning styles. Provide opportunities for independent study and project-based learning, allowing Children to explore their passions and interests.

Create a classroom environment that is calming and supportive. Minimize distractions, use soft lighting, and consider incorporating calming elements such as plants or calming music. Be mindful of sensory sensitivities when planning classroom activities. Consider providing quiet spaces or sensory breaks for students who become overwhelmed. Above all, cultivate a culture of empathy and understanding within the classroom.

FOR CAREGIVERS in general, patience, understanding, and acceptance are essential qualities. Indigo Children are often misunderstood, labeled as "difficult" or "problematic." By providing a supportive and nurturing environment, you can help them develop self-esteem and resilience. Celebrate their unique talents and abilities and encourage them to pursue their passions. Help them to develop coping mechanisms for dealing with their sensitivities. This could involve mindfulness practices, deep breathing exercises, or spending time in nature.

Remember, the journey of supporting an Indigo Child is a marathon, not a sprint. There will be challenges, setbacks, and moments of frustration. But by focusing on creating a supportive and understanding environment, you can help these extraordinary Children thrive and realize their full potential. ***Their sensitivities are not weaknesses; they are gifts that, when nurtured, can contribute significantly to the world. They are visionaries, empathetic leaders, and creative thinkers. By fostering their development, we are not only helping individual Children, but we are also nurturing the very qualities our world so desperately needs.*** The future depends on their growth, their understanding, and their ability to contribute their unique perspectives to the world. The journey is a collaboration; a shared effort between the Child, their parents, educators, and wider community, all working together to help them blossom into their truest selves. It's a testament to the interconnectedness of all things, a reminder that we all have a role to play in supporting each other's growth and development on this collective journey.

UNDERSTANDING
Twin Flames

Understanding the profound bond between twin flames requires a nuanced approach, going beyond the romantic ideal often portrayed in popular culture. While the intense connection and undeniable magnetism are undeniable aspects of the twin flame dynamic, it's crucial to recognize this relationship as a catalyst for profound spiritual growth, often intertwined with the Starseed journey.

The term "twin flame" itself evokes a sense of mystical unity, suggesting two halves of a single soul, destined to reunite and embark on a shared spiritual odyssey. Unlike soulmates, who share a deep connection based on shared values, life experiences, and complementary energies, twin flames are believed to possess a more intense, almost telepathic bond, often described as an "instant recognition" or a feeling of "coming home." This isn't to diminish the profound significance of soulmate relationships; rather, it highlights the unique intensity and transformative potential inherent within the twin flame dynamic.

The concept of twin flames isn't confined to a single cultural background; its echoes resonate across various spiritual traditions and belief systems. In some ancient cultures, the idea of a divine counterpart, a mirror reflecting one's soul's essence, has existed for millennia. These narratives often depict a challenging, transformative journey of reunion, mirroring the often turbulent yet ultimately enriching experience many twin flame connections embody. Understanding these varied cultural perspectives broadens our understanding of the universal longing for connection and wholeness that underlies the twin flame concept.

The characteristics of a twin flame relationship are often intensely marked. The initial encounter frequently involves an overwhelming sense of recognition, a feeling of knowing the other person on a profound level, despite limited prior interaction. This intense connection often transcends the physical plane, manifesting as shared dreams, synchronicities, or a deep intuitive understanding of each other's thoughts and feelings. Communication can feel effortless, even telepathic, with a shared understanding that bypasses the need for extensive explanation. This doesn't mean the relationship is devoid of challenges; in fact, the very intensity of the connection can amplify conflicts and disagreements, pushing both individuals to confront deep-seated wounds and limiting beliefs.

This process of confrontation isn't a sign of incompatibility; rather, it's a crucial aspect of the transformative journey. *Twin flames often act as mirrors, reflecting each other's shadow selves, the hidden aspects of personality we tend to avoid confronting. This mirroring effect can be painful, triggering unresolved traumas and emotional patterns.* However, by facing these challenges head-on, both individuals have the opportunity for profound self-discovery and healing. This intense introspection is often accompanied by periods of separation, allowing each twin to process their experiences and integrate the lessons learned. *These separations aren't necessarily indicative of failure; they often represent crucial moments of individual growth, ultimately paving the way for a deeper and more harmonious union.*

The spiritual growth fostered within a twin flame connection is profound and complex.

Both individuals are challenged to confront their deepest fears, limiting beliefs, and unresolved emotional wounds. The relationship acts as an accelerator for spiritual evolution, pushing both partners to confront their ego, overcome self-doubt, and embrace their authentic selves. This often manifests as an intensified exploration of spiritual practices, such as meditation, energy work, or exploring different spiritual traditions. The shared spiritual journey allows for a mutual understanding and support that transcends the limitations of conventional relationships. The shared exploration of spiritual practices often leads to a deeper connection to universal energies and a more profound sense of interconnectedness.

The connection between twin flames and Starseeds is particularly significant. Many believe that Starseeds, having incarnated on Earth with a specific mission or purpose, often find their twin flames are fellow Starseeds, sharing a similar cosmic origin and spiritual destiny. This shared background contributes to the intense bond and shared understanding that characterize twin flame relationships. The experiences of Starseeds, often involving heightened sensitivity, psychic abilities, and a strong sense of intuition, resonate profoundly with the unique characteristics of twin flame connections. This shared experience forms a foundation of mutual understanding and support, allowing both partners to navigate the complexities of their earthly journey with greater grace and ease.

It is important to differentiate the twin flame connection from other intense relationships, as the term is sometimes misused or misinterpreted. The twin flame connection is not simply a passionate romantic entanglement; it's a spiritually significant journey of transformation and growth. While the romantic element can be present, the core of the twin flame dynamic lies in the shared spiritual journey and mutual support in navigating life's challenges. This distinction emphasizes that the intensity of the connection is not solely rooted in romantic desire but rather in a shared spiritual destiny and the profound interconnectedness of two souls. Misinterpretations and unrealistic expectations can lead to disappointment and disillusionment; understanding the true nature of the twin flame connection fosters a more realistic and fulfilling experience.

The journey of a twin flame connection is rarely straightforward; it often involves periods of intense joy and deep sorrow, moments of profound understanding and inexplicable conflict. This rollercoaster of emotions is a crucial part of the process, challenging both individuals to confront their shadow selves and emerge stronger and more spiritually evolved. The challenges aren't merely obstacles to overcome; they are opportunities for growth, pushing each individual to expand their consciousness and develop deeper compassion and understanding. Embracing the journey's complexities fosters resilience, adaptability, and a deeper appreciation for the transformative power of the twin flame relationship.

The concept of twin flames is not simply a romantic ideal; it's a pathway to self-discovery and spiritual growth. The journey requires courage, self-awareness, and a willingness to confront one's vulnerabilities. It challenges the ego, allowing for the emergence of a more authentic and compassionate self. This self-discovery is not solely a personal journey; it's a shared odyssey, with both individuals supporting each other's evolution. The shared experiences forge a bond that transcends the limitations of conventional relationships, deepening the sense of connection and mutual support. This shared journey fosters a heightened sense of purpose, a sense of belonging in the universe, and a deeper appreciation for the spiritual aspect of life.

Understanding the twin flame connection requires moving beyond simplistic notions of romantic love. It is a profound spiritual odyssey characterized by intense connection, shared purpose, and transformative growth. The challenges inherent in the relationship are not obstacles to be overcome, but rather opportunities for profound self-discovery and spiritual evolution.

The connection often involves periods of separation and reconciliation, allowing for individual growth and the integration of lessons learned. For Starseeds, the twin flame connection is often a critical part of their spiritual journey, amplifying their purpose and providing mutual support in navigating their unique path. The ultimate goal is not merely a romantic union but a shared spiritual journey toward greater self-awareness, fulfillment, and a deeper connection with the universe.

The intensity of the experience is a catalyst for profound transformation, pushing individuals to confront their shadow selves and emerge stronger, more compassionate, and more spiritually connected. This journey of self-discovery, guided by the energy and synergy of a twin flame connection, is a testament to the boundless potential for growth and transformation that lies within each soul.

THE DYNAMICS
Of Twin Flame Relationships

The journey of a twin flame connection is rarely a linear progression; it's more akin to a dynamic dance, a complex interplay of attraction, repulsion, mirroring, and ultimately, a striving towards union. Understanding the dynamics of this relationship requires acknowledging the cyclical nature of its progression, often characterized by periods of intense connection interspersed with necessary separations. These separations, far from signifying failure, serve as crucial periods for individual growth and self-discovery.

During these times apart, each individual processes the intense energy of the connection, confronts their own inner shadows, and integrates the lessons learned during periods of proximity.

One of the most significant challenges in twin flame relationships is the intense mirroring effect. Each individual serves as a mirror reflecting the other's unhealed wounds, unexamined beliefs, and unresolved emotional patterns. ***This mirroring can be incredibly painful, triggering deep-seated insecurities and vulnerabilities. It may manifest as intense arguments, disagreements over seemingly insignificant issues, or a persistent feeling of being misunderstood.*** However, this mirroring is not inherently negative; it's a powerful catalyst for self-awareness and personal growth. By facing the reflections of their own imperfections, each individual has the opportunity to heal old wounds, release limiting beliefs, and embrace their authentic selves. The discomfort of the mirroring process forces a necessary introspection, pushing each partner toward self-improvement and personal transformation.

EFFECTIVE COMMUNICATION is fundamental in navigating the complexities of a twin flame relationship. While the initial connection may feel effortless and intuitive, misunderstandings and miscommunications can easily arise as the relationship deepens. Open and honest communication, even during periods of conflict, is vital for maintaining a healthy connection. This requires a willingness to listen deeply, to empathize with the other person's perspective, and to express one's own needs and feelings with vulnerability and compassion. It's important to approach disagreements not as personal attacks, but as opportunities for growth and understanding. Learning to communicate effectively fosters a deeper level of intimacy and strengthens the bond between the two individuals. The ability to navigate conflict constructively is a crucial skill in fostering a healthy and enduring twin flame connection.

SELF-AWARENESS plays a crucial role in successfully navigating the intense energy of a twin flame relationship. This involves a willingness to look inward, to acknowledge one's own shadow aspects, and to take responsibility for one's thoughts, feelings, and actions. It requires cultivating self-compassion, understanding that everyone carries imperfections and vulnerabilities. The journey necessitates a commitment to personal growth, a willingness to confront personal challenges, and a dedication to healing past wounds. Through self-reflection and introspection, each individual can develop a deeper understanding of their own patterns and behaviors, ultimately fostering a more balanced and healthy relationship. Self-awareness is the foundation upon which a strong and enduring twin flame connection can be built.

MUTUAL GROWTH is essential for the long-term success of a twin flame relationship. The relationship itself is not a destination but a journey of continuous learning and development. Both individuals should support each other's personal growth, celebrating each other's successes and offering compassion during times of struggle.

This means respecting each other's individual paths, supporting each other's goals, and creating space for individual expression. It's about fostering a reciprocal environment where both individuals feel empowered to evolve and grow both independently and together. A healthy twin flame connection is one in which both individuals are actively engaged in their personal development, inspiring and supporting each other along the way.

The concept of twin flames encompasses a variety of dynamics and expressions. While the archetypal image might portray a romantic pairing, the reality is far more nuanced. Some twin flame relationships manifest as intensely romantic partnerships, characterized by deep love, passion, and unwavering devotion. Others may take the form of platonic friendships, characterized by profound understanding and unwavering support. Still others exist in a space beyond easy categorization, blending elements of both romantic and platonic connection. Regardless of the specific expression, the underlying dynamic remains consistent: an intense spiritual connection, a powerful sense of recognition, and a shared journey of transformation and growth. It is important to acknowledge this spectrum of expression and resist the temptation to impose rigid definitions on a relationship that defies easy classification.

The twin flame journey is not always easy; periods of intense challenge and seeming

incompatibility are often part of the process. During these times, it is crucial to maintain a sense of perspective and remember the underlying purpose of the connection. The conflicts and difficulties are not signs of failure but opportunities for growth, pushing both individuals to confront their shadow selves and emerge stronger and more spiritually evolved. It is essential to maintain patience, compassion, and an unwavering belief in the transformative potential of the connection. The challenges should be viewed as stepping stones, each one offering valuable lessons and leading toward a deeper, more profound understanding of oneself and the relationship. The journey is not a race, but a gradual unfolding of consciousness and connection.

The role of surrender in a twin flame relationship is often underestimated. *Surrender does not imply passivity or resignation; it involves releasing control, trusting the divine timing of the universe, and accepting the ebb and flow of the connection.* It requires a willingness to let go of preconceived notions, expectations, and attachments to specific outcomes.

Surrender fosters a sense of peace and acceptance, allowing each individual to be present in the moment and to trust in the unfolding of the relationship. It's about releasing resistance to the divine plan, embracing the unpredictable nature of the journey, and trusting in the ultimate outcome. This trust allows for a deeper connection to the divine, strengthening the bond between the individuals and supporting their shared journey. Navigating the challenges of a twin flame relationship requires courage, self-awareness, and a deep commitment to personal growth. It's a journey that requires both individuals to confront their vulnerabilities, release limiting beliefs, and embrace their authentic selves. The process is often challenging, marked by periods of intense emotion, confusion, and even pain. However, it's through these challenges that the deepest transformations occur.

The rewards of persevering through the difficulties are beyond measure, leading to profound self-discovery, increased spiritual awareness, and a deeply fulfilling relationship that transcends the limitations of conventional partnerships. ***The journey is a profound evidence of the power of love, growth, and the transformative potential of the human spirit.*** The ultimate goal is not simply a romantic union, but a shared spiritual evolution, a journey of self-discovery that leads to a profound connection with the divine and a deepened understanding of one's place within the universe.

TWIN FLAMES
And Spiritual Awakening

The intense energy inherent in a twin flame connection often serves as a powerful catalyst for spiritual awakening. This isn't merely a matter of heightened emotions; it's a profound acceleration of the soul's evolution, a rapid expansion of consciousness that can feel both exhilarating and overwhelming. The very presence of the twin flame acts as a mirror, reflecting back aspects of ourselves we may have consciously or unconsciously suppressed. This mirroring effect, while sometimes painful, forces us to confront our shadow self –those hidden parts of our personality that we tend to avoid. The process of integration, of acknowledging and embracing these shadow aspects, is a cornerstone of spiritual growth. By confronting our fears, insecurities, and limiting beliefs, we begin to dismantle the walls we've built around our hearts and minds, creating space for greater self-acceptance and spiritual expansion.

This accelerated spiritual growth often manifests in several ways.

Individuals may experience a **sudden surge in intuition**, feeling a heightened connection to their inner wisdom. They may become more **attuned to the subtle energies** around them, developing a greater sensitivity to the emotional states of others. Some may find themselves drawn to practices like meditation, yoga, or energy healing, seeking deeper connection to their spiritual selves. **Creative pursuits** may blossom, as the intensified energy finds expression in art, music, writing, or other forms of self-expression. **Dreams** may become more vivid and symbolic, offering insights into the unconscious mind and the unfolding spiritual journey. *There's often a profound shift in perspective, a sense of expanded awareness that extends beyond the personal realm, into a deeper understanding of the interconnectedness of all things.*

The challenges inherent in a twin flame relationship often serve as critical junctures in this spiritual growth. Periods of separation, conflict, and intense emotional upheaval, while painful, provide invaluable opportunities for self-reflection and inner work. These challenges force us to confront our own patterns of behavior, our attachments, and our limiting beliefs. The process of navigating these difficulties, of learning to communicate effectively, and of cultivating compassion and empathy, strengthens our inner resilience and fosters emotional maturity. It is within these crucible experiences that we shed old skins, releasing outdated patterns and embracing healthier ways of being.

Synchronicities play a significant role in the twin flame journey.

These seemingly coincidental events – unexpected meetings, recurring numbers, meaningful messages appearing at just the right moment – often serve as guiding signs, highlighting the interconnectedness of the universe and confirming the validity of the path. These synchronicities can be deeply reassuring, offering a sense of guidance and support amidst the often tumultuous journey. They are gentle nudges from the universe, offering reassurance and reminding us that we are not alone in this process. They can help us to remain focused on our path, even when faced with setbacks or doubt. Paying attention to these synchronicities helps to develop a deeper sense of trust in the divine timing of the universe and empowers us to surrender to the unfolding of the journey.

The intense energy of a twin flame connection can, at times, feel overwhelming. It's not unusual to experience periods of intense emotional ups and downs, fluctuating between feelings of euphoria and despair. This emotional intensity is a testament to the profound nature of the connection, a reflection of the accelerated spiritual growth occurring. However, it's vital to manage this energy effectively, employing tools like meditation, grounding techniques, and mindful self-care to prevent burnout and maintain a sense of equilibrium. Learning to navigate these intense emotions is a crucial aspect of the spiritual journey. It's a lesson in emotional mastery, teaching us to accept and process a wider range of feelings with greater clarity and compassion. Developing self-regulation techniques allows us to harness the immense energy of the twin flame connection for personal growth rather than feeling overwhelmed by it.

The ultimate purpose of a twin flame connection is not necessarily a romantic partnership in the traditional sense, although that can certainly be part of the journey. ***The deeper purpose lies in mutual spiritual growth, a shared journey of self-discovery that leads to a deeper understanding of oneself, the universe, and one's place within the cosmic scheme.*** It's a catalyst for expanding consciousness, awakening dormant potential, and fostering a deeper connection to the divine. The relationship can challenge us to confront our deepest fears, to break free from limiting beliefs, and to embrace our authentic selves. The process is often tumultuous, but the rewards are immeasurable, leading to a richer, more fulfilling life lived with a greater sense of purpose and meaning.

The journey of spiritual awakening within a twin flame relationship is unique to each individual pair. There's no single template, no prescribed path to follow. The experiences will vary widely, dependent upon the individual's unique spiritual journey, their prior experiences, and their willingness to embrace the challenges and opportunities presented. What unites all twin flame experiences is the intense energy of the connection, the potent catalyst for spiritual growth, and the profound transformation that arises from navigating the complexities of the relationship. Trusting the process, surrendering to the divine timing, and embracing the lessons along the way is vital in navigating this deeply transformative journey.

The process of self-discovery within a twin flame relationship is often accompanied by a profound deepening of self-compassion.

The intense mirroring effect can expose our vulnerabilities, highlighting our insecurities and past wounds. However, instead of judgment, this process encourages a gentle self-acceptance. We begin to see our imperfections not as flaws, but as integral parts of our being, integral to our growth and evolution. This self-compassion extends not only to ourselves but also to our twin flame, understanding their journey and struggles with greater empathy. The ability to hold space for both oneself and the other, with kindness and compassion, is a defining characteristic of a successful twin flame connection. This fosters a sense of mutual understanding and support, enabling both individuals to navigate the challenges with resilience and grace.

The journey continues beyond the initial stages of spiritual awakening. As we integrate the lessons learned, we move towards a deeper understanding of our purpose within the larger context of the universe. The twin flame connection can serve as a guide, illuminating our unique path and providing the support needed to manifest our dreams. It becomes a partnership not only in love and companionship, but in shared purpose and co-creation. This collaboration extends beyond the personal realm, inspiring us to contribute our gifts and talents to the world in meaningful ways, fulfilling our individual and collective destinies. The twin flame connection acts as a beacon, illuminating the path towards a life lived with intention, authenticity, and purpose.

The transformative power of a twin flame relationship extends beyond the personal realm. As we evolve spiritually, we naturally become more sensitive to the needs of others and more attuned to the interconnectedness of all living things. This heightened sensitivity fosters a deeper sense of empathy and compassion, encouraging us to contribute to a better world. We may find ourselves drawn to humanitarian efforts, social justice initiatives, or environmental activism, motivated by a desire to use our newfound spiritual awareness to make a positive impact on the world. This desire to serve is a natural outgrowth of spiritual awakening within the context of a twin flame connection, demonstrating the broader implications of this profound personal journey. The twin flame relationship, therefore, becomes a force for good, not just in the lives of the two individuals involved, but in the broader community and the world.

Finally, remember that the twin flame journey is a continuous process of growth and transformation, an ongoing unfolding of consciousness. There will be highs and lows, periods of intense connection and periods of separation. Embrace the journey, learn from the challenges, and trust in the divine timing of the universe.

The ultimate goal is not a perfect union free of conflict, but a deepened understanding of oneself, one's twin flame, and one's place in the grand scheme of existence. It's a journey of self-discovery, spiritual awakening, and the unfolding of one's highest potential, a testament to the boundless power of love and the transformative potential of the human spirit. The journey's destination is not a specific point in space and time, but rather the continuous expansion of consciousness and love.

HEALING AND INTEGRATION
In Twin Flame Relationships

Healing and integration are not merely optional add-ons in a twin flame journey; they are the very bedrock upon which a sustainable and fulfilling connection is built. The initial intensity, the undeniable pull, the almost overwhelming sense of recognition – these are the initial sparks. But the true work, the transformative alchemy, lies in the conscious effort to heal past wounds and integrate the fragmented selves that often precede the meeting of twin flames. This process requires courage, vulnerability, and a profound commitment to self-awareness.

Many individuals entering a twin flame connection carry significant emotional baggage from past relationships, traumas, or unresolved family dynamics. These unhealed wounds often manifest as patterns of behavior, limiting beliefs, and emotional reactivity that can significantly impact the twin flame dynamic. For example, a past experience of betrayal might lead to deep-seated mistrust, making it difficult to fully embrace the vulnerability inherent in a twin flame relationship. Similarly, unresolved Childhood trauma might manifest as emotional instability or difficulty establishing healthy boundaries. Recognizing and addressing these underlying issues is crucial for fostering a healthy and balanced connection.

One of the most potent tools for healing and integration is self-compassion. The intensity of the twin flame connection often acts as a magnifying glass, illuminating our shadow selves – those aspects of ourselves we tend to repress or deny. This can be incredibly challenging, triggering feelings of shame, guilt, or inadequacy.

However, it is precisely through embracing these shadow aspects with self-compassion that true healing begins. Instead of judging ourselves harshly for our imperfections, we must learn to accept them as integral parts of our journey, as opportunities for growth and transformation. This involves practicing self-forgiveness, releasing self-criticism, and cultivating a sense of self-acceptance, understanding that our imperfections are not flaws but simply part of our unique human experience.

This self-compassion must extend to our twin flame. The mirroring effect inherent in the connection often means we see reflected back our own flaws and insecurities, sometimes amplified. It's crucial to avoid projecting our own issues onto our partner, instead practicing empathy and understanding. Attempting to "fix" our twin flame or expecting them to meet our unmet needs will only hinder the healing process. We must remember that they are on their own unique journey, and their struggles are equally valid. Holding space for their emotions, even when challenging, is an act of profound compassion and a cornerstone of a healthy twin flame relationship.

Effective communication is another vital element in the healing and integration process. This goes beyond simple verbal exchanges; it involves actively listening to understand, rather than to respond. It means creating a safe and supportive space where both individuals feel comfortable expressing their thoughts, feelings, and vulnerabilities without fear of judgment. This often requires setting healthy boundaries, learning to express needs clearly and assertively, and actively practicing empathy. ***Misunderstandings and conflicts are inevitable, but learning to navigate them constructively, through open and honest dialogue, is key to building resilience and strengthening the bond.*** For instance, engaging in active listening, where one partner fully focuses on the other's words without interrupting, and then summarizes their understanding to ensure clarity is a powerful tool for resolving conflict.

The process of healing often involves confronting deep-seated fears and insecurities. This can be particularly challenging in the context of a twin flame relationship, where the intensity of the connection can amplify these anxieties. Facing these fears requires courage and a willingness to step outside of one's comfort zone. This might involve engaging in introspection, journaling, therapy, or other self-exploration practices to understand the root causes of these fears and develop strategies for managing them. Techniques like shadow work, where one consciously confronts and integrates their shadow self, can be particularly effective in this process. This can take years, requiring patience and unwavering self-belief.

Many find that engaging in practices that promote self-regulation are incredibly helpful in navigating the sometimes intense emotional landscape of a twin flame connection. These practices, such as meditation, yoga, breathwork, or spending time in nature, help to calm the nervous system, center the mind, and ground the body. Regular engagement with these practices fosters inner peace and resilience, allowing individuals to better cope with periods of emotional upheaval. They offer a haven, a way to connect with the inner self, and to restore balance amidst the turbulence of the journey. The choice of self-regulatory practice is personal; the goal is to find what resonates most and to create a sustainable self-care routine.

Furthermore, seeking professional support can significantly enhance the healing and integration process. A therapist or counselor can provide a neutral and objective perspective, helping individuals to identify and address underlying issues, develop healthy coping mechanisms, and improve communication skills. They can also offer guidance in navigating difficult periods and provide support during times of conflict or separation. It's important to remember that seeking professional help is a sign of strength, not weakness, and it can be an invaluable tool in building a strong and sustainable relationship.

The integration process is not a linear one. It's a journey marked by ups and downs, periods of progress and periods of regression. There will be times when old wounds resurface, requiring renewed attention and care. It's crucial to approach this process with patience, self-compassion, and unwavering dedication to the journey. Recognizing that setbacks are a natural part of the process prevents discouragement and reinforces the commitment to ongoing personal growth.

Throughout this journey, the focus should always remain on mutual growth and understanding. The twin flame connection is not just about romantic love; it's about shared spiritual growth, mutual support, and co-creation of a life filled with purpose and meaning.

This involves embracing the lessons learned during challenging periods, using them as catalysts for deeper self-awareness and strengthening the bond between the two individuals. By prioritizing mutual respect, empathy, and unconditional love, the twin flame partnership can blossom into a powerful force for good in each other's lives, and ultimately, in the world at large. The journey is not about reaching a perfect destination but about the continuous evolution of both individuals, supported by the deep connection they share. It is a testament to the enduring power of love and the potential for profound human transformation. The commitment to ongoing growth and self-reflection is essential for a fulfilling and enduring twin flame relationship.

The ultimate reward is not merely a romantic union, but a profound expansion of consciousness and a life lived with authentic purpose and unconditional love.

THE PURPOSE
Of Twin Flame Unions

Beyond the intensely personal journey of healing and integration lies a deeper, more expansive purpose inherent in the twin flame connection. While the individual transformation is undeniably crucial, the true significance of this union often extends far beyond the confines of the dyad. Twin flames, in their interconnectedness and shared spiritual evolution, possess a unique potential to contribute to a larger collective consciousness shift, acting as catalysts for positive change in the world. This contribution doesn't necessarily involve grand gestures or public pronouncements; it's often expressed in the subtle, yet profound, ways in which their relationship ripples outwards, touching the lives of those around them.

The very nature of a twin flame connection – the intense mirroring, the shared spiritual journey, the profound understanding – fosters a heightened level of empathy and compassion. This amplified capacity for empathy is not simply contained within the relationship; it naturally extends to the wider world. Twin flames often find themselves compelled to engage in acts of service, driven by a deep-seated desire to alleviate suffering and contribute to the betterment of humanity. This might manifest as volunteering for a cause close to their hearts, advocating for social justice, or simply offering a listening ear and unwavering support to those in need.

The shared energy and intensified intuition that characterize the twin flame dynamic can often lead to a heightened sense of purpose and a clearer understanding of their unique contributions to the collective good.

Their journey of self-discovery and healing can also serve as an inspiration to others. The vulnerability, the honesty, and the willingness to confront shadow aspects inherent in the twin flame journey can resonate deeply with others struggling with similar challenges. The very act of sharing their experiences, even in subtle ways, can offer hope and guidance to others navigating their own paths of self-discovery and spiritual growth. The strength and resilience demonstrated in overcoming obstacles within the relationship can become a beacon of hope for others facing their own personal struggles. This indirect impact, the ripple effect of their journey, contributes significantly to raising collective consciousness and fostering a culture of healing and understanding.

The accelerated spiritual evolution experienced by twin flames is another key aspect of their broader purpose. The intensity of the connection often acts as a catalyst for profound spiritual growth, pushing both individuals to confront their deepest fears and insecurities, to embrace their authentic selves, and to unlock their full potential. This accelerated growth isn't solely for their personal benefit; it also contributes to the evolution of consciousness on a larger scale. As they evolve, their expanded awareness and heightened vibrational frequency have a ripple effect, influencing those around them and contributing to a more harmonious and interconnected world. Their journey becomes a living testament to the power of love, transformation, and spiritual growth, inspiring others to embark on their own journeys of self-discovery.

The concept of "service" in the context of a twin flame union extends beyond traditional notions of volunteering or charitable work. It encompasses a broader spectrum of contributions, including the simple act of embodying love, compassion, and understanding in their daily interactions. By cultivating a life of authenticity and integrity, twin flames act as living examples of the potential for human connection and spiritual growth. They model healthy relationships, embodying empathy, respect, and unconditional love. This modeling becomes a powerful form of service, silently influencing the world through their actions and their presence. Their relationship itself becomes a testament to the power of love and transformation, inspiring others to strive for deeper connection and personal growth.

Furthermore, the creativity and innovation often fostered by a twin flame connection can contribute significantly to society. The shared energy, heightened intuition, and mutual inspiration can lead to breakthroughs in various fields, ranging from the arts and sciences to business and social innovation. This creative synergy, born from the intense bond between twin flames, can produce remarkable results, benefiting not only the individuals themselves but also the wider community. This contribution to collective advancement underscores the far-reaching impact of the twin flame dynamic, extending beyond the personal realm and into the sphere of societal progress. This creative energy can manifest in many forms, from innovative business ventures that promote social good to artistic expressions that inspire reflection and empathy.

However, it's crucial to understand that the purpose of a twin flame union isn't about imposing their beliefs or forcing transformation on others. It's about being authentically themselves, allowing their love, compassion, and spiritual growth to radiate outwards naturally. *Their role is not to preach or to judge, but to inspire through their own evolution and conscious embodiment of their values.* Their influence is a subtle, organic process, radiating outward from their core, impacting others in countless unseen ways. This quiet influence is arguably the most powerful form of service, demonstrating the potential for personal transformation to have a far-reaching collective impact.

The challenges and difficulties inherent in the twin flame journey are not obstacles to be avoided, but rather opportunities for growth and deeper understanding. These challenges, when navigated with integrity and compassion, contribute to the overall purpose of the union, refining their individual and collective abilities to serve a higher purpose. The struggles they overcome, the lessons learned, and the wisdom gained become integral parts of their collective contribution to the world. This constant process of refinement and growth ensures that their service to humanity is continuous and ever-evolving. They are constantly learning, growing, and adapting their service to meet the ever-changing needs of the world around them.

Ultimately, the purpose of a twin flame union is complex and deeply significant. It's a journey of profound personal transformation that extends to encompass a larger collective impact, contributing to a world of greater love, compassion, understanding, and spiritual evolution. ***The role of twin flames is not simply to find personal happiness, but to contribute to the elevation of consciousness for the collective good, to be a beacon of hope and inspiration, and to embody the potential for human connection and transformation.*** It's a powerful and transformative calling, a sacred responsibility, and a journey of profound significance within the larger cosmic tapestry. The journey is a testament to the unifying power of love and the potential for individual growth to create a ripple effect of positive change throughout the world. The ultimate impact of their union is not solely measurable in quantifiable terms but in the countless, often unseen, ways it touches the lives of others and contributes to a more conscious and compassionate world. The enduring legacy of a true twin flame connection lies not just in their shared love, but in the ripple of positive change they inspire in all they touch.

GUIDED MEDITATIONS
For Energy Healing

Embarking on a journey of self-discovery often involves confronting deep-seated emotional wounds and energetic imbalances. The transformative power of energy healing, coupled with the focused intention of guided meditation, offers a potent path to release these blockages and unlock your inherent potential. These meditations are designed to be gentle yet effective, guiding you through a process of self-awareness, energy clearing, and chakra balancing.

Remember, consistency is key; even short daily practices can yield profound results over time. Find a quiet space where you can relax without interruption. Sit comfortably, either on a cushion or in a chair, with your spine straight but not rigid. Close your eyes gently and allow your breath to become slow and even. Before starting each meditation, take a few moments to center yourself, connecting with your breath and allowing any tension to melt away.

MEDITATION 1: Grounding and Centering

This meditation focuses on establishing a strong connection to the earth, grounding your energy, and creating a sense of centeredness. Begin by focusing your attention on your breath. Notice the rise and fall of your chest or abdomen.

With each inhale, imagine drawing in calm, grounding energy, and with each exhale, releasing any tension or anxiety.

Visualize roots extending from your base chakra, deep into the earth, anchoring you firmly in place. Feel the earth's energy flowing up through your roots, filling you with a sense of stability and security.

This energy is supportive, nourishing, and deeply calming. Allow this feeling of grounding to permeate your entire being. Spend several minutes basking in this sense of grounded stability, allowing yourself to simply be present in this moment. When you're ready, gently bring your awareness back to your breath, then slowly open your eyes.

MEDITATION 2:
Chakra Balancing

This meditation is designed to help you balance and harmonize your seven main chakras. Begin by visualizing your root chakra, located at the base of your spine, as a vibrant crimson red.

Imagine this energy center spinning smoothly and effortlessly, radiating a warm, grounding energy. Now, move your focus to your sacral chakra, located just below your navel, visualizing it as a bright orange. Feel the creative life force energy pulsating within this center.

Continue this process, moving sequentially through your solar plexus chakra (yellow),

Your Heart Chakra (Green),

Your Throat Chakra (Light Blue)

Your Third-Eye Chakra (Indigo),

Your Crown Chakra (Violet).

With each chakra, imagine it spinning smoothly, radiating its unique color and energy. If you notice any blockages or imbalances, visualize a gentle stream of white light flowing through the chakra, cleansing and purifying it. Spend several minutes focusing on each chakra before moving to the next, allowing the energy to flow freely and harmoniously throughout your entire energy system. When you're ready, gently bring your awareness back to your breath, then slowly open your eyes.

MEDITATION 3:
Energy Clearing

This meditation helps clear away stagnant or negative energy, leaving you feeling refreshed and renewed. Begin by taking a few deep breaths, grounding yourself in the present moment.

Visualize a brilliant white light surrounding your body, acting as a protective shield.

As you inhale, imagine this light expanding, encompassing your entire aura.

As you exhale, visualize any stagnant or negative energy being drawn out of your body and into the white light.

See this energy transforming into pure, positive energy as it merges with the white light. Continue this process for several minutes, allowing the white light to cleanse and purify your energy field.

Feel the lightness and clarity that follows as the negative energy dissipates. When you're ready, gently bring your awareness back to your breath, then slowly open your eyes.

MEDITATION 4:
Self-Compassion *and* Forgiveness

This meditation promotes self-acceptance and forgiveness, vital elements in personal transformation. Begin by sitting comfortably, closing your eyes, and taking several deep, grounding breaths.

Bring to mind any situations or experiences that have caused you pain or suffering.

Acknowledge these experiences without judgment, recognizing that they have shaped you, and that you are not defined by them.

Visualize yourself as a Child, experiencing the pain you carry. Offer compassion and understanding to your younger self. Speak words of kindness and reassurance, acknowledging their pain and offering forgiveness for any perceived shortcomings.

Imagine embracing your younger self, holding them close and offering comfort. Then, ***extend this compassion and forgiveness to your present self.***

Accept yourself unconditionally, acknowledging your strengths and weaknesses without judgment. Forgive yourself for past mistakes and imperfections.

Know that you are worthy of love, compassion, and acceptance. Spend several minutes basking in this feeling of self-compassion and forgiveness. When you're ready, gently bring your awareness back to your breath, then slowly open your eyes.

MEDITATION 5:
Connecting *with* Your Higher Self

This meditation guides you to connect with your higher self, accessing your inner wisdom and guidance. Begin by settling into a comfortable seated position, closing your eyes, and taking several deep breaths to center yourself.

Visualize a bright, radiant light above your head, representing your higher self. Imagine this light descending, filling you with warmth, love, and wisdom. Feel this energy merging with your own, connecting you to your deepest essence.

Ask your higher self any questions you may have, allowing the answers to come to you intuitively. Listen to your inner voice, trusting your intuition and inner guidance. ***You may receive messages through images, feelings, or words.***

Simply allow yourself to receive the wisdom and guidance that is offered. Spend several minutes basking in this connection, allowing your higher self to fill you with love, light, and clarity. When you're ready, gently bring your awareness back to your breath, then slowly open your eyes.

MEDITATION 6:
Affirmations for Transformation

This meditation incorporates positive affirmations to support your personal transformation. Begin by sitting comfortably, closing your eyes, and taking several deep, centering breaths. Choose three to five affirmations that resonate with your goals for transformation.

Examples include:

"I am strong, capable, and resilient,"

"I am worthy of love and happiness,"

"I am open to new possibilities,"

"I am embracing my authentic self,"

"I release all limiting beliefs."

Repeat each affirmation several times, visualizing yourself embodying the qualities expressed. Feel the energy of the affirmation flowing through your body, creating positive changes within you.

Focus on the feeling of the affirmation, rather than just the words themselves.

Let these positive statements permeate your being, strengthening your resolve and supporting your journey of transformation. Spend several minutes repeating the affirmations, allowing them to sink deep into your subconscious mind. When you're ready, gently bring your awareness back to your breath, then slowly open your eyes.

INTEGRATING MEDITATION
Into Your Daily Life

The benefits of regular meditation extend far beyond the practice itself. Consistent practice helps to cultivate a greater sense of self-awareness, inner peace, and emotional resilience. It can help reduce stress and anxiety, improve sleep quality, and boost overall well-being. Over time, you may find that your intuition strengthens, your creativity expands, and your ability to navigate life's challenges increases. As you integrate these meditations into your daily life, remember to approach your practice with patience and compassion. Don't judge yourself for any wandering thoughts or feelings that may arise during meditation. Simply acknowledge them and gently redirect your focus back to your breath or your chosen visualization.

The key is consistency, not perfection. Even a few minutes of daily practice can have a significant positive impact on your life. Experiment with different techniques and find what works best for you. The most important aspect is to create a dedicated space for self-reflection and inner exploration. Through consistent practice and mindful awareness, you will begin to experience the transformative power of meditation and energy healing. Embrace this journey of self-discovery and allow yourself to grow and evolve into your most authentic self. The path to transformation is an ongoing process, and these meditations are designed to support you every step of the way. Remember, your inner strength and resilience are your greatest assets in this transformative journey.

JOURNALING PROMPTS FOR SELF-DISCOVERY

Journaling offers a powerful avenue for self-discovery, particularly for those on a path of spiritual exploration and transformation. It's a space where you can unpack your experiences, confront limiting beliefs, and unearth the wisdom residing within your own heart.

Unlike the structured focus of meditation, journaling allows for free-flowing expression, a process that can be both cathartic and illuminating. The prompts below are designed to facilitate this process, guiding you towards a deeper understanding of yourself and your place in the universe. Remember, there are no right or wrong answers; the value lies in the process of honest self-reflection.

Let's begin with prompts focusing on your unique experiences as a potential Starseed. This isn't about adhering to a rigid definition, but rather exploring aspects of your life that resonate with the essence of this concept – heightened sensitivity, profound connection to nature, a yearning for something more, and a sense of otherness.

PROMPTS EXPLORING STARSEED THEMES:

1. **INTENSE EMOTIONS AND HEIGHTENED SENSITIVITY:** Describe a time when your emotional sensitivity felt overwhelming or challenging.

What triggered the intense emotions?

How did you respond?

What did you learn from this experience about managing your sensitivity?

Can you identify patterns in your emotional reactions?

This exploration allows you to understand the depth and breadth of your emotional landscape, recognizing your sensitivity not as a weakness, but as a powerful tool for empathy and connection.

2. **CONNECTION TO NATURE:** Describe your relationship with nature.

Do you feel a deep affinity for the natural world?

What are your favorite natural settings?

When in nature, what emotions or feelings arise within you?

Recall a specific instance where you felt a powerful connection to nature; describe the experience in vivid detail. This inquiry delves into a profound connection often associated with Starseed experiences, revealing how nature nurtures your soul and offers respite from worldly concerns.

3. **YEARNING FOR SOMETHING MORE:** Reflect on feelings of longing, a sense that there's something deeper or more significant to your life than what you currently experience.

What is this "something more"?

Where does this feeling originate?

What steps have you taken to address this yearning?

This prompt acknowledges the intuitive pull toward a greater purpose, a feeling many associate with a soul's unique journey.

4. **SENSE OF OTHERNESS:** Describe moments where you felt different or out of place among others.

Did you ever feel like you didn't belong?

How did this feeling affect you?

What were the triggers for this sense of otherness?

How have you learned to accept and embrace your uniqueness?

This exploration acknowledges that feeling different can be a source of both challenge and strength, leading to a deeper sense of self-acceptance.

5. **DREAMS AND VISIONS:** Describe any recurring dreams or visions you experience.

What symbols or imagery stand out?

What feelings or emotions accompany these dreams?

Do you believe these experiences hold any significance?

This exploration taps into the realm of intuition and symbolism, opening doors to subconscious wisdom and greater self-understanding.

Beyond the specific Starseed themes, let's move to broader prompts that encourage self-reflection and personal growth:

PROMPTS FOR BROADER SELF-DISCOVERY:

6. **CORE VALUES AND BELIEFS:** Identify your core values and beliefs.

What principles guide your decisions and actions?

Are there any conflicts between your values and your actions?

How can you live more authentically aligned with your values?

This exploration illuminates the inner compass that guides your life, revealing areas where you are living in harmony with your truest self and areas where adjustments may be necessary.

7. **PAST LIFE EXPERIENCES:** If you believe in past lives, explore this aspect of your journey.

What feelings, memories, or insights have you gained from reflecting on potential past lives?

How might these experiences inform your current life path?

Even if you don't have clear memories, consider what experiences might have shaped your current personality or tendencies. This foray into past life exploration can offer powerful insights into recurring themes and patterns in your life journey, suggesting deeper meanings and understandings.

8. **PERSONAL STRENGTHS AND WEAKNESSES:** Identify your greatest strengths and weaknesses.

How do these strengths and weaknesses manifest in your daily life?

What are the origins of these characteristics?

How can you utilize your strengths more effectively, and how can you address and transform your weaknesses?

This exploration invites honesty and self-compassion, allowing you to build upon strengths and work towards personal growth in areas of challenge.

9. **UNRESOLVED EMOTIONAL ISSUES:** Reflect on any unresolved emotional issues or traumas.

What feelings or experiences are you still grappling with?

What steps could you take to begin healing and processing these challenges?

What support might you need?

This exploration touches upon the importance of acknowledging and addressing past hurts, highlighting the significance of self-compassion and healing.

10. **GRATITUDE AND APPRECIATION:** Identify aspects of your life you're truly grateful for.

What people, experiences, or possessions bring you joy and fulfillment?

This practice shifts the focus towards abundance and appreciation, cultivating a sense of positivity and contentment.

11. **GOALS AND ASPIRATIONS:** Reflect on your personal goals and aspirations.

What do you hope to achieve in the next year, five years, or ten years?

What steps can you take to move closer to realizing these goals?

This exploration aligns your aspirations with concrete actions, creating a pathway towards manifest destiny and a more fulfilling life.

12. **SPIRITUAL GROWTH:** Reflect on your spiritual journey.

What lessons have you learned?

What challenges have you overcome?

What is your understanding of your spiritual purpose?

How can you further your spiritual growth?

This self-examination considers the wider arc of your spiritual journey, fostering a deeper understanding of your connection to the cosmos and to a universal energy.

Interpreting And Utilizing Journal Insights

After completing these prompts, take time to reflect on the patterns and themes that emerge. Look for recurring emotions, beliefs, or experiences that offer clues about your core identity and life purpose. Don't shy away from difficult or uncomfortable insights. These are often the most valuable lessons, leading to profound self-awareness and personal transformation.

As you gain clarity, create actionable steps to integrate these insights into your daily life. Journaling can be a powerful tool not only for self-discovery, but for creating lasting positive change. Regular journaling will support you in recognizing your inherent worth, embracing your unique path, and becoming the most authentic and empowered version of yourself.

The journey of self-discovery is ongoing; embrace the process and allow yourself to grow and evolve. The insights gained through these journaling prompts are a compass guiding you toward a deeper understanding of yourself and your place in the vast cosmic tapestry.

AFFIRMATIONS FOR SELF EMPOWERMENT

Building upon the introspective journey of self-discovery through journaling, we now turn our attention to another potent tool for transformation: affirmations. Affirmations are positive statements that, when repeated consistently, can reprogram our subconscious mind, shifting our beliefs and ultimately shaping our reality.

For those who identify with the Starseed experience, affirmations can be particularly powerful in navigating the unique challenges and embracing the inherent gifts of heightened sensitivity and a deep connection to the universe.

The process of affirmation isn't merely about positive thinking; it's about consciously choosing thoughts and beliefs that align with the empowered self you wish to become. It's about rewriting the narrative of your life, replacing limiting beliefs with empowering ones.

For Starseeds, who often grapple with feelings of otherness or a sense of not quite belonging, affirmations can offer a crucial tool for self-acceptance and integration. They act as a counterbalance to the internal dialogue that might otherwise perpetuate feelings of isolation or inadequacy.

The key to effective affirmation lies in consistency and belief. It's not enough to simply repeat the phrases; you must genuinely believe in their truth, even if you don't fully feel it at first. Think of affirmations as seeds you're planting in the fertile ground of your subconscious. With consistent nurturing—repeating the affirmations daily, preferably in a quiet, meditative state—these seeds will sprout and blossom, transforming your inner landscape.

The following affirmations are designed specifically to address common challenges faced by Starseeds, fostering self-empowerment, and celebrating your unique gifts. Feel free to adapt them to resonate deeply with your personal experience, using them as a springboard for creating your own personalized affirmations.

Remember, the power of affirmation comes from your genuine commitment to the process and your belief in your own inherent worth.

AFFIRMATIONS FOR EMBRACING YOUR SENSITIVITY:

- **I embrace** my heightened sensitivity as a gift, allowing me to deeply connect with myself and the world around me.

- **My sensitivity** is a source of strength, enabling me to empathize with others and offer profound compassion.

- **I honor** my emotions, allowing myself to feel them fully without judgment or self-criticism.

- **I trust** my intuition and inner wisdom, knowing that it guides me towards my highest good.

- **I am capable** of managing my energy effectively, setting boundaries to protect myself from overwhelm.

- **I am surrounded** by a loving and supportive community that cherishes my unique qualities.

- **I am resilient** and resourceful, capable of navigating life's challenges with grace and strength.

- **I am grateful** for my profound emotional depth, for it enhances my capacity for love and connection.

- **I release** any feelings of shame or guilt associated with my sensitivity, embracing my authentic self.

- **I choose** to see my sensitivity as a superpower, enabling me to experience life with vibrant intensity.

AFFIRMATIONS FOR OVERCOMING FEELINGS OF OTHERNESS:

- **I am a unique** and valuable individual, worthy of love and belonging.

- **I embrace** my individuality, celebrating my differences and uniqueness.

- **I am deeply connected** to the universe and to a greater purpose. I belong here, on this planet, and I am fulfilling my soul's mission. I am surrounded by kindred spirits who understand and accept me for who I am.

- **I am part of a larger cosmic family**, connected to beings of light and love.

- **I am safe** and supported, both within and without.

- **I release** any feelings of isolation or loneliness, choosing to embrace connection and community.

- **I am divinely guided** and protected, always on the right path for my soul's growth.

- **I am perfectly imperfect**, and my imperfections are part of what makes me beautiful and unique.

AFFIRMATIONS FOR CULTIVATING SELF-LOVE AND ACCEPTANCE:

- **I love and accept myself** unconditionally, flaws and all.

- **I am worthy** of happiness, joy, and abundance in all areas of my life.

- **I forgive myself** for past mistakes and choose to move forward with compassion and grace.

- **I am grateful** for my journey, for it has shaped me into the beautiful soul I am today.

- **I nurture** my body, mind, and spirit with love and care.

- **I am confident** in my ability to overcome any challenges that arise.

- **I am strong**, resilient, and capable of achieving anything I set my mind to.

- **I believe** in my potential and trust in my ability to manifest my dreams.

- **I am filled** with self-compassion, understanding and forgiving myself unconditionally.

- **I radiate** love, joy, and peace into the world, creating a ripple effect of positive energy.

AFFIRMATIONS FOR CONNECTING WITH YOUR HIGHER PURPOSE:

- **I am aligned** with my soul's mission and purpose.

- **I am guided** by my intuition and inner wisdom, leading me to my highest potential.

- **I trust** that the universe is supporting me every step of the way. I am open to receiving divine guidance and support.

- **I am grateful** for the opportunities that come my way to fulfill my purpose.

- **I am confident** and fearless in pursuing my passions and dreams. I am making a positive difference in the world, leaving a legacy of love and light.

- **I am a powerful** creator, manifesting my desires with ease and grace.

- **I am living** a life of purpose and meaning, fulfilling my soul's contract.

- **I am deeply grateful** for the journey of self-discovery and the blessings it brings.

Creating Your Own Personal Affirmations

While these affirmations offer a valuable starting point, the most powerful affirmations are those you create yourself. To craft your own personalized affirmations, consider the areas of your life where you wish to experience transformation. Identify limiting beliefs that are holding you back and rephrase them into positive, empowering statements. Keep your affirmations short, concise, and positive, focusing on the desired outcome rather than the problem.

For example, if you struggle with self-doubt, instead of saying "I am not good enough," you might affirm "I am capable, competent, and worthy of success." If you feel overwhelmed by your sensitivity, you might choose an affirmation like "I manage my energy with grace and ease, choosing responses that empower me." Remember, the effectiveness of your affirmations depends on your belief in their truth and your commitment to repeating them consistently.

Choose affirmations that resonate deeply with your heart and soul. Speak them aloud with conviction and feeling, visualizing the desired outcome as you do so. Write them down and place them where you'll see them frequently throughout the day. Integrate them into your daily routine, repeating them first thing in the morning and last thing at night, or even throughout the day whenever you feel the need for a boost of positive energy.

Self-empowerment is an ongoing journey.

Affirmations are a valuable tool to support you on this path, helping you to cultivate self-love, embrace your unique gifts, and live a life aligned with your highest potential. Combine the introspective power of journaling with the positive reinforcement of affirmations, and you'll unlock a potent synergy for profound transformation. Remember, you are worthy, you are capable, and you are divinely guided on your unique Starseed journey.

Visualization Techniques for Manifestation

Building on the transformative power of affirmations, we now delve into the potent practice of visualization – a technique that allows us to harness the creative power of our minds to manifest our desires. Visualization, in essence, is the art of creating vivid mental images of our goals, engaging all our senses to experience them as if they are already real. This isn't mere daydreaming; it's a conscious and intentional act of shaping our reality through the power of focused intention. For Starseeds, with their inherent sensitivity and intuitive connection to the universe, visualization can be a particularly powerful tool for aligning with their higher purpose and manifesting a life that reflects their unique gifts.

The effectiveness of visualization hinges upon several key elements: clarity, belief, and consistent practice. Clarity involves forming a precise mental picture of what you want to manifest. The more detailed and vivid your visualization, the stronger the energetic imprint you create in your subconscious mind. Instead of vaguely envisioning "success," visualize the specific aspects of success you desire – the feeling of accomplishment, the tangible results, the impact on your life and the lives of others. See yourself achieving your goal, hear the sounds associated with it, smell the accompanying scents, taste the sweetness of victory, and feel the physical sensations related to your accomplishment. Engage all five senses to paint a vibrant and realistic picture in your mind's eye.

Belief is equally crucial. Doubt acts as a powerful counterforce to the energy you are directing towards your manifestation. To cultivate belief, remember the progress you've already made on your spiritual journey. Recall instances where your intuition guided you, your sensitivity provided profound insights, and your connection to the universe brought unexpected opportunities. These experiences serve as proof of your inherent ability to manifest your desires. Believe in your capacity to create the reality you envision. Affirm your belief through positive self-talk, reminding yourself of your inherent power and the universe's support.

Consistent practice is the key to transforming your visualizations from fleeting thoughts into tangible realities.

Schedule regular visualization sessions, even if it's just for a few minutes each day.

Find a quiet space where you can relax and focus without distractions. Create a sacred space – perhaps using crystals, candles, essential oils – that enhances your ability to connect with your inner self and the universal energy that supports your manifestations.

The visualization process itself begins with relaxation. Deep, conscious breathing techniques can help to calm your mind and body, preparing you for a state of heightened receptivity. Once you are relaxed, begin by visualizing your desired outcome in as much detail as possible. Feel the emotions associated with achieving your goal – joy, excitement, gratitude. Engage your senses fully, experiencing the sight, sound, smell, taste, and touch of your manifested reality. Hold this vision in your mind for several minutes, allowing yourself to fully immerse in the experience.

However, the journey isn't always smooth sailing. Challenges may arise – doubts may creep in, distractions might pull your focus, and frustration might tempt you to give up. These challenges are simply opportunities for growth. When doubt arises, acknowledge it without judgment. Remind yourself of your past successes, your inherent resilience, and the power of your focused intention. When distractions occur, gently redirect your attention back to your visualization. When frustration sets in, take a break, reconnect with your breath, and reaffirm your commitment to the process.

Perseverance is key; your unwavering commitment to your vision will ultimately determine your success.

Visualizing for specific areas of your life can be immensely powerful. For example, if you seek to enhance your relationships, visualize yourself surrounded by loving, supportive individuals. See their faces, hear their voices, feel the warmth of their connection. If you wish to improve your health, visualize your body radiating vitality and strength. See your cells renewing, your energy flowing freely, your body functioning optimally. If your goal involves financial abundance, visualize yourself surrounded by prosperity. See the abundance flowing into your life, feel the sense of security and freedom it brings. Be specific in your visualization; the more detail you include, the more effective it will be.

Let's explore some practical techniques to enhance your visualization practice:

Guided Meditations: Numerous guided meditations are available online or through apps, designed specifically for manifestation.

These meditations often incorporate soothing music, calming voices, and specific instructions to help you achieve a deeper state of relaxation and enhance your ability to visualize. Experiment with different guided meditations to find those that resonate with you.

Vision Boards: Create a physical representation of your goals by creating a vision board. Gather images, quotes, and objects that represent your desired outcome and arrange them on a board. Spend time each day gazing at your vision board, reaffirming your commitment to your goals and reinforcing your visualizations.

Affirmations during Visualization: Combine the power of affirmations with visualization. As you visualize your desired outcome, repeat affirmations that support your goals and reinforce your belief in your ability to manifest them.

Scripting: Write down a detailed description of your desired reality as if it has already manifested. Use present tense and vivid language, engaging all your senses. Read your script regularly, allowing yourself to fully immerse in the experience.

Mind Mapping: Utilize mind mapping to break down your goals into smaller, more manageable steps. This can help to clarify your vision and create a roadmap for your manifestation journey.

Remember, the visualization process is a journey of self-discovery and empowerment.

It's a practice that requires patience, perseverance, and unwavering belief in your ability to shape your reality.

For Starseeds, this journey is especially profound, allowing you to connect with your inherent cosmic potential and manifest a life that truly reflects your unique gifts. Embrace your sensitivity, trust your intuition, and allow yourself to be guided by the universe's infinite wisdom. The power to create your reality lies within you. Embrace it, and watch as your visualizations transform into tangible realities. The path to manifestation is a continuous process, one that requires consistent practice and unwavering belief. As you refine your visualization techniques and deepen your connection to your inner self, you will become increasingly adept at manifesting your desires.

Remember to practice self-compassion, acknowledging that setbacks are part of the process. Maintain a positive outlook, focusing on the progress you've made rather than dwelling on any perceived failures. The universe supports your journey, providing guidance and opportunities along the way. Trust in this divine support, and continue to refine your visualization skills, creating the life you were destined to live. The power to transform your reality is within your grasp; seize it and create a future aligned with your deepest desires and your unique Starseed journey.

Creating a Sacred Space *for* Self-Reflection

Creating a sacred space for self-reflection is not about opulent furnishings or extravagant décor; it's about cultivating an environment that fosters inner peace, facilitates profound connection, and nurtures the soul. This sanctuary, however humble, becomes a crucible for transformation, a place where the echoes of the universe resonate within your being, amplifying your inherent Starseed gifts. The process of creating this space is as personal and unique as you are, a reflection of your individual journey and a testament to your commitment to self-discovery.

Begin by selecting a location that feels inherently peaceful and private. This might be a corner of your bedroom, a quiet nook in your living room, or even a secluded spot outdoors. The key is to find a place where you feel undisturbed, free from external distractions that could disrupt your meditative state. Consider the natural light in the space; soft, diffused light is generally more conducive to relaxation. If natural light isn't readily available, opt for soft, warm lighting, perhaps through candles or a Himalayan salt lamp. The subtle, warm glow of these lights creates a calming ambiance, enhancing the meditative atmosphere. Avoid harsh fluorescent or overhead lighting that can feel sterile and jarring.

Once you've selected your location, begin to curate the ambiance. This is where your creativity and intuition will shine. The sensory experience plays a crucial role in shaping the atmosphere of your sacred space. Consider the use of aromatherapy, incorporating essential oils that resonate with your personal energy and promote relaxation and introspection. Lavender, chamomile, sandalwood, and frankincense are all excellent choices known for their calming and grounding properties. You might use a diffuser to gently disperse the scent, or simply add a few drops to a cotton ball placed discreetly in the room. Experiment with different blends to discover the scents that best enhance your meditative state and support your spiritual journey.

The power of crystals is another potent tool for enhancing your sacred space. Each crystal holds a unique vibrational energy, capable of amplifying certain intentions and promoting specific energetic states. Amethyst, for instance, is renowned for its calming and purifying qualities, facilitating spiritual connection and promoting inner peace. Selenite is known for its cleansing properties, clearing away stagnant energy and creating a space conducive to meditation and self-reflection. Clear quartz is a versatile crystal that amplifies the energy of other crystals and enhances overall energy flow. Choose crystals that resonate with your personal needs and intentions, placing them strategically within your sacred space to enhance its transformative power. Remember, the placement of the crystals isn't arbitrary; intuitively position them in the areas where you feel their energy is most beneficial.

Sound is another powerful element to consider. Gentle, calming music can create a soothing backdrop for your meditation. Nature sounds, such as flowing water or birdsong, can be especially effective in promoting relaxation and connecting you with the natural world. Alternatively, the absence of sound – a tranquil silence – can be equally powerful, allowing you to tune into your inner voice and connect with your deepest self. Experiment with different soundscapes to determine what most enhances your experience.

The visual aspect of your sacred space is equally important.

Surround yourself with objects that inspire peace, tranquility, and spiritual growth. This could include nature-inspired artwork, inspirational quotes, or personal mementos that hold significance for your journey. Avoid cluttering the space; maintaining a sense of order and simplicity promotes a sense of calm. Consider the colors you use within your sacred space. Soft, muted tones, such as blues, greens, and lavenders, tend to be soothing and conducive to relaxation. ***Avoid bright, harsh colors that might feel stimulating rather than calming.***

Incorporating elements from nature can deeply enhance the experience. Place fresh flowers, potted plants, or even natural stones within your space. Nature has an innate ability to ground and center us, providing a tangible connection to the earth's energy. The living presence of plants also helps purify the air, adding to the overall sense of well-being.

Creating a sacred space isn't about perfection; it's about intention.

Even a simple, unadorned space can become a profound sanctuary when imbued with your focused intention. The act of dedicating a space to self-reflection and spiritual growth is itself a powerful act of commitment.

Consider adding elements that represent your personal spiritual journey.

This may involve incorporating symbols or images that resonate with your beliefs, spiritual practices, or Starseed lineage. For instance, you might include celestial imagery, feathers, or other symbolic objects that hold personal meaning. This personal touch makes your sacred space truly unique and reflects your individual path.

Remember, your sacred space is a living, evolving entity.

As your spiritual journey progresses, your needs and preferences may change, and so may your sacred space. Allow it to evolve organically, reflecting the ever-changing landscape of your inner world. Regularly cleanse and energize your sacred space to maintain its purity and potency. You can do this by smudging with sage or palo santo, using sound therapy, or simply expressing gratitude for the sacredness of this space.

Creating a sacred space for self-reflection is an act of self-love and self-care. It's a commitment to nurturing your inner world, honoring your spiritual journey, and cultivating a sanctuary where you can connect with your higher self and the universe's boundless wisdom. This sanctuary provides a refuge from the demands of the external world, a place where you can retreat, recharge, and reconnect with your true essence. Embrace this journey of creating your personal haven; the rewards are immeasurable. *The energy you invest in creating this space will be magnified tenfold, transforming it into a powerful catalyst for profound self-discovery and spiritual transformation.* The time spent within this sacred space is an investment in your well-being, a nurturing act that will ripple outwards, enriching all aspects of your life. It is within this carefully cultivated haven that you will discover the depth of your own inner wisdom and connect with the vast cosmic energies that flow through you. The journey of self-discovery is a lifelong pursuit, and this sacred space will become a steadfast companion on your path, a refuge where you can continually reconnect with your true essence, embrace your Starseed heritage, and manifest the reality that aligns with your deepest desires. Make it a space of unwavering support, constant growth, and profound peace.

The Greater Cosmic Perspective

Embracing a cosmic perspective isn't about abandoning your earthly reality; it's about expanding your awareness to encompass a far grander narrative. It's about understanding that your individual journey, with its unique joys and challenges, is inextricably interwoven with the cosmic tapestry of existence. Each experience, each moment of growth and each period of seeming stagnation, contributes to the intricate beauty of the universe's unfolding story. The seemingly random events, the synchronicities, the seemingly insurmountable obstacles—all are threads in this vast, interconnected web.

Consider the vastness of space, the countless galaxies swirling in an infinite expanse. Within this immensity, our planet, a tiny speck of dust, holds life in its breathtaking diversity. And within that life, you exist, a unique expression of consciousness, a vibrant spark of the divine. This perspective isn't meant to diminish your personal experience; rather, it magnifies it, placing it within a context of unimaginable grandeur. Your struggles become not isolated incidents but opportunities for growth within the grand cosmic dance. Your joys become expressions of universal abundance, reflecting the boundless creativity inherent in the cosmos.

This sense of interconnectedness extends beyond the purely physical. Consider the unseen energies that permeate all things, the subtle vibrational frequencies that connect every living being. We are all participants in a grand cosmic symphony, each contributing our unique note to the harmonious whole. Your thoughts, emotions, and actions ripple outwards, influencing not only those around you but the fabric of reality itself. This understanding fosters a deep sense of responsibility and empowers you to use your energy consciously, to create a reality that aligns with your highest aspirations and contributes positively to the whole.

The concept of Starseeds, often associated with heightened sensitivity and an innate understanding of the interconnectedness of all things, naturally fits within this cosmic perspective. Your unique sensitivities are not flaws but rather antennas, tuning you into the subtle energies that permeate the universe. Your intuitive insights are not mere whims of fancy but whispers of cosmic wisdom, guiding you toward your purpose and illuminating your path. Embrace these sensitivities as gifts, nurturing them and utilizing them to navigate your journey with grace and understanding.

Furthermore, embracing a cosmic perspective fosters a profound sense of humility. The sheer immensity of the universe puts our individual concerns into a broader perspective. The challenges that seem insurmountable in our daily lives appear less daunting when viewed against the backdrop of cosmic time and space. This isn't about dismissing your struggles; it's about gaining a more balanced perspective, recognizing the temporary nature of challenges and cultivating resilience in the face of adversity.

The journey of self-discovery, therefore, is not a solitary endeavor, but a collaborative journey with the universe itself. The cosmos is not a passive observer but an active participant, guiding and supporting you on your path. The synchronicities, the unexpected opportunities, the seemingly serendipitous encounters—all are manifestations of this collaborative process. Embrace these moments as guidance, trusting that the universe is conspiring to support your growth and expansion.

Continuous learning and growth are integral to this cosmic journey. The universe is in a constant state of expansion and evolution, and so too should you be. Embrace new experiences, challenge your beliefs, and remain open to the unexpected. Each new piece of knowledge, each new experience, expands your understanding of yourself and your place within the cosmic tapestry. There is no end to this journey, no final destination, only continuous unfolding and expansion. The pursuit of knowledge and wisdom becomes a lifelong commitment, a testament to your willingness to grow and evolve.

This broader perspective also helps us understand and navigate the concept of suffering. Suffering, in this cosmic context, is not simply something to be avoided but a catalyst for growth and transformation. It's a crucible in which the soul is refined, its strengths tested and honed. The challenges we face, the setbacks we experience, are opportunities to learn, to grow, and to deepen our understanding of ourselves and the universe. Through these experiences, we develop resilience, compassion, and a deeper connection to the human spirit. The seemingly harsh lessons life imparts serve to strengthen our resolve and deepen our empathy.

The sense of belonging that emerges from this cosmic perspective is profound and transformative. You are not alone in your journey; you are connected to every living being, every star, every galaxy.

You are part of something immense, something beautiful, something awe-inspiring. This understanding fosters a sense of purpose, a sense of meaning, and a deep appreciation for the interconnectedness of all life. Your individual experiences contribute to the overall harmony of the universe, and you are an essential part of this intricate and beautiful dance.

This cosmic perspective is not a belief system to be adopted; it is a way of seeing the world, a lens through which you can view your life and your experiences with greater clarity and understanding. It is a journey of continuous exploration and expansion, a deepening of your connection to the universe and to your own inner wisdom.

It's a path of self-discovery that unfolds throughout your life, continually revealing new layers of understanding and enriching your experience. Embrace this journey with curiosity, courage, and a deep sense of wonder. Allow yourself to be swept away by the immensity and beauty of the cosmos, and in doing so, you will discover the profound beauty and significance of your own unique existence within it. Let the universe guide you, and allow yourself to be guided by the infinite wisdom that flows through all things. The journey is the destination, and the journey is shared. You are not alone.

NAVIGATING
The Challenges Of Being A Starseed

The cosmic journey, while exhilarating and filled with potential, is not without its trials. Starseeds, with their heightened sensitivities and often profound intuitive abilities, frequently find themselves navigating a world that doesn't always understand, or even acknowledge, their unique experiences. This can lead to feelings of isolation, misunderstanding, and even overwhelm. But these challenges are not insurmountable; they are, in fact, opportunities for growth and deepening self-awareness. Learning to navigate these difficulties is a crucial part of embracing your cosmic journey.

One of the most significant challenges faced by Starseeds is energy sensitivity. This heightened sensitivity can manifest in many ways, from feeling deeply affected by the emotions of others to experiencing physical discomfort in crowded or energetically charged environments. Imagine being a finely tuned instrument, exquisitely sensitive to every vibration in the surrounding orchestra. While this sensitivity allows for a deep connection with the universe and a profound empathy for others, it can also lead to exhaustion and overwhelm. Learning to manage this sensitivity is paramount to maintaining well-being.

Practical strategies for managing energy sensitivity include establishing clear boundaries. Learning to say "no" to commitments that drain your energy is vital. Prioritizing solitude and engaging in activities that replenish your energy are equally crucial. This might involve spending time in nature, meditating, practicing yoga, or engaging in creative pursuits that allow for self-expression and emotional release. Consider the concept of an "energy shield" – a metaphorical protective layer that you consciously create to safeguard yourself from overwhelming external energies. Visualize a bubble of light surrounding you, deflecting negative or draining energies. This is not about shutting yourself off from the world, but about creating a healthy space for yourself to manage your energy effectively.

Another significant hurdle for Starseeds is often the presence of limiting beliefs. These beliefs, often ingrained from childhood or societal conditioning, can hinder your progress and prevent you from fulfilling your cosmic purpose. These beliefs might manifest as self-doubt, feelings of inadequacy, or a belief that you are not worthy of happiness or success. Identifying and challenging these beliefs is a crucial step in breaking free from their constraints.

Journaling can be an invaluable tool in this process. By writing down your thoughts and feelings, you can begin to identify recurring patterns and underlying beliefs that may be holding you back. Cognitive Behavioral Therapy (CBT) techniques can also be incredibly effective in challenging and reframing negative thought patterns. This involves consciously identifying and replacing negative self-talk with more positive and realistic affirmations. Remember, your beliefs are not immutable; they are choices, and you have the power to change them.

Cultivating healthy relationships is also a crucial aspect of navigating the challenges of being a Starseed. Because of their heightened sensitivity and often unconventional perspectives, Starseeds may find it challenging to connect with others on a deep level. It's important to remember that you don't need to compromise your authenticity to connect with others. Instead, seek out individuals who appreciate and understand your unique perspective, who resonate with your values, and who support your growth. Surrounding yourself with a supportive community can provide a sense of belonging and alleviate feelings of isolation.

Self-care is not a luxury; it's a necessity for Starseeds. Their heightened sensitivity makes them particularly susceptible to stress and burnout. Prioritizing self-care practices is essential for maintaining both physical and mental well-being. This might include regular exercise, a balanced diet, sufficient sleep, and engaging in activities that bring you joy and relaxation.

Incorporating mindfulness practices, such as meditation or deep breathing exercises, can help to calm the mind and reduce stress. Remember that self-care is an act of self-love, a recognition of your inherent worth and a commitment to your overall well-being.

Stress management is another crucial component of navigating the challenges inherent in being a Starseed. Developing effective stress-management techniques is essential for preventing burnout and maintaining a sense of balance. These techniques can include anything from regular exercise and mindfulness practices to spending time in nature or engaging in creative pursuits. Exploring alternative therapies, such as acupuncture or energy healing, may also be beneficial for managing stress and promoting overall well-being. Remember that finding the right techniques is a process of experimentation; what works for one person may not work for another. The key is to find what resonates with you and consistently incorporates it into your daily life.

It is crucial to remember that your journey is unique. There is no one-size-fits-all approach to navigating the challenges of being a Starseed. What works for one individual may not work for another.

Be patient with yourself, and trust your intuition to guide you toward the path that is right for you. Seeking support is not a sign of weakness; it is a sign of strength. Don't hesitate to reach out to others for help, whether it be friends, family, therapists, or spiritual mentors. There are many people who understand and support your journey. Remember, you are not alone.

The challenges you face are opportunities for growth, for deepening your self-awareness, and for strengthening your connection to the universe. Embrace your unique sensitivities, challenge your limiting beliefs, and cultivate healthy relationships. Prioritize self-care and stress management, and remember that seeking support is a sign of strength. Your journey is a testament to your resilience, your courage, and your unwavering commitment to your cosmic purpose.

Trust in your path, and know that you are exactly where you are meant to be, on your uniquely beautiful and transformative cosmic journey. The universe supports you, and you are never truly alone. Embrace the magnificence of your being, the profoundness of your purpose, and the extraordinary power residing within you. You are a Starseed, a beacon of light, and your journey is one of profound significance.

Let your light shine brightly!

The path ahead may seem daunting at times, filled with moments of doubt and uncertainty. But remember, even the darkest nights are followed by dawn. The challenges you encounter are not meant to break you;

they are designed to strengthen you, to refine you, to prepare you for the incredible potential that lies ahead. Each obstacle overcome, each lesson learned, brings you closer to the fulfillment of your cosmic purpose.

Your sensitivity, often perceived as a weakness, is your greatest strength. It allows you to connect with the universe on a profound level, to tap into the infinite wisdom that flows through all things.

Embrace this sensitivity, nurture it, and utilize it to guide your decisions, to inspire your actions, and to create a life that aligns with your deepest values.

The feeling of isolation, a common experience for Starseeds, is a temporary illusion. You are connected to something far greater than yourself, to a universal consciousness that embraces and supports you in your journey. Seek out like-minded individuals, build a supportive community, and allow yourself to be vulnerable and authentic with those who understand and appreciate you for who you are.

Finally, remember that your cosmic journey is a lifelong process of growth and evolution. There is no end point, no final destination. The journey itself is the destination, a continuous unfolding of your potential, a constant expansion of your consciousness. Embrace the unknown, welcome the unexpected, and trust in the infinite wisdom of the universe to guide you on your path. You are a powerful, unique being, and your journey is one of incredible beauty and significance. Embrace it, and let your light shine brightly.

Finding Your Place *in the* Universe

Finding your unique place within the vast cosmic tapestry is a journey of self-discovery, a process of unfolding your inherent potential and aligning with your deepest purpose. As a Starseed, you carry within you a unique energetic signature, a vibrational frequency that resonates with the universal symphony of existence. Understanding this signature, this intrinsic essence, is key to finding your rightful place within the grand cosmic design.

This isn't about fitting into a pre-ordained mold or conforming to societal expectations. Instead, it's about embracing your individuality, celebrating your differences, and recognizing the immense value you bring to the world.

Your unique gifts, your heightened sensitivities, your intuitive abilities – these are not flaws or weaknesses; they are the very instruments through which you contribute to the collective evolution of consciousness.

The universe is not a static entity; it is a dynamic, ever-evolving system, a vast ocean of energy constantly in motion. Each Starseed, with their unique vibrational frequency, plays a vital role in this cosmic dance. You are not merely a passive observer; you are an active participant, a co-creator of reality, contributing to the ever-unfolding symphony of existence.

Imagine the universe as a magnificent orchestra, composed of countless instruments, each with its unique timbre and tone. Some instruments are loud and bold, others soft and subtle; some play rhythmic beats, others soaring melodies. Each instrument contributes to the overall harmony, and the absence of even one would diminish the richness and complexity of the music. Similarly, each Starseed, with their unique gifts and talents, contributes to the overall harmony of the universe. Your unique contribution is essential, and your absence would leave a void in the cosmic symphony.

One of the most profound ways Starseeds contribute to the collective evolution of consciousness is through their heightened sensitivity. This sensitivity allows you to perceive subtle energies, to empathize deeply with others, and to intuitively grasp the underlying interconnectedness of all things. This heightened awareness enables you to be a conduit for compassion, understanding, and healing within your community and the world at large. You are like a finely tuned antenna, receiving and transmitting information on multiple levels – physical, emotional, mental, and spiritual.

Your intuition, that inner voice that guides you, is not merely a hunch or a gut feeling; it is a direct line to your higher self, a connection to the universal intelligence that permeates all of existence. Trusting your intuition is paramount to finding your place in the universe. When faced with a decision, take a moment to quiet your mind, to center yourself, and to listen to the gentle whisper of your inner voice. Pay attention to the subtle feelings, the intuitive nudges, the inner knowing that guides you toward your true path.

This doesn't mean ignoring logic or reason; rather, it's about integrating intuition with rational thought, creating a harmonious blend of both. Your intuition acts as a compass, guiding you towards opportunities for growth and aligning you with your higher purpose. Your logic then assists you in navigating the practical aspects of pursuing those opportunities. The two work in perfect harmony, leading to more holistic and aligned decision making.

Following your path, your unique purpose in this life, requires courage. It requires the willingness to step outside of your comfort zone, to embrace the unknown, and to trust in the divine guidance that is always available to you. This path may not always be easy; it may involve challenges, setbacks, and periods of doubt. But remember that these are not roadblocks; they are opportunities for growth, for learning, and for strengthening your resolve.

The universe conspires to support those who are committed to their path. As you move forward with intention and trust, synchronicities will appear, opportunities will present themselves, and people and resources will emerge to aid you in your journey. This is not merely coincidence; it is a manifestation of the universe's support, a testament to the power of intention and alignment with your higher purpose.

Living authentically is essential to finding your place in the universe. This means being true to yourself, expressing your unique gifts and talents, and living in alignment with your values. It means refusing to compromise your integrity for the sake of fitting in or pleasing others. Authenticity is a beacon of light that attracts like-minded individuals, creating a supportive community of souls who understand and appreciate your unique journey.

Authenticity requires vulnerability, a willingness to share your true self with the world, even when it's uncomfortable. Vulnerability is not weakness; it is strength, a testament to your courage and your willingness to embrace your imperfections. By sharing your authentic self, you invite others to do the same, creating a ripple effect of authenticity that transforms the world.

Embracing your unique identity as a Starseed is not about seeking validation from others; it is about recognizing your inherent worth and embracing your divine purpose. You are a unique expression of the universe, a beautiful and powerful being with a unique contribution to make. Your presence on this planet is not accidental; it is a purposeful act, a contribution to the greater cosmic plan.

The feeling of belonging, of being connected to something larger than yourself, is a fundamental human need. As a Starseed, you may have felt a sense of otherness, a feeling of not quite fitting in.

However, understand that your unique qualities are not meant to isolate you; they are meant to connect you to a community of like-minded individuals. Seek out those who understand your experiences, who resonate with your sensitivities, and who appreciate your unique perspectives.

Finding your tribe, your spiritual family, is an integral part of your journey. They are fellow travelers on the cosmic path, individuals who share your passion for spiritual growth, who understand the challenges you face, and who offer support and encouragement along the way. These connections provide a sense of belonging, a feeling of being seen, understood, and appreciated for who you truly are.

Remember that you are never truly alone on your cosmic journey.

The universe is alive with energy, pulsating with life, and supporting you every step of the way. Trust in the guidance you receive, embrace your challenges as opportunities for growth, and allow your light to shine brightly. Your unique contribution to the universe is essential, and your journey is a testament to the incredible power and beauty that resides within you. Your place in the universe is not something you find; it is something you create, through living authentically, following your intuition, and embracing your unique and powerful self. You are a Starseed, a beacon of light, and your journey is just beginning. Embrace the vastness of your potential, and allow your light to illuminate the world. The universe awaits your contribution, and the cosmos sings your song.

CONTINUING
Your Spiritual Growth

Continuing your spiritual journey as a Starseed is not a destination, but a lifelong odyssey of self-discovery and unfolding. It's a path of continuous learning, evolving understanding, and deepening connection with the cosmic energies that flow through you. The initial steps of recognizing your Starseed nature are only the beginning; true growth lies in actively cultivating your spiritual potential and nurturing the unique gifts you bring to the world.

One of the most crucial aspects of continued growth is a commitment to lifelong learning. This isn't simply about accumulating knowledge; it's about cultivating a thirst for understanding, a deep yearning to explore the mysteries of the universe and your place within it. This involves engaging with diverse perspectives, challenging your preconceived notions, and remaining open to new insights and experiences. Explore different spiritual traditions, delving into ancient wisdom and contemporary teachings alike. Read books, attend workshops, and listen to lectures that broaden your understanding of consciousness, energy, and the interconnectedness of all things.

Self-reflection is another invaluable tool on your spiritual path. Take time for introspection, journaling, and meditation. Regularly assess your beliefs, values, and actions, asking yourself how they align with your higher purpose and your intuitive guidance.

Consider keeping a spiritual journal to track your insights, experiences, and lessons learned. This journal serves not just as a record of your journey, but as a powerful instrument for self-discovery and growth. Pay attention to recurring themes, patterns, and synchronicities that emerge. These often provide invaluable clues to understanding your deeper purpose and navigating your life's journey.

Don't underestimate the power of meditation as a means of deepening your connection to your inner self and the universe. Regular meditation allows you to quiet the mental chatter, still the racing thoughts, and access a space of inner peace and clarity. In this space, you become more receptive to your intuition, your connection to the divine, and the subtle energies that surround you. Explore different meditative techniques to find what best suits your personality and preferences. Guided meditations, visualization exercises, and mindfulness practices can all be valuable tools for enhancing your spiritual awareness.

Seeking support from like-minded individuals is crucial to your ongoing spiritual development. Surround yourself with a community of individuals who understand your unique experiences and sensitivities. This could involve joining a spiritual group, attending workshops, or connecting with others online who share your Starseed beliefs. Sharing your journey with others creates a sense of belonging, validation, and mutual support. The collective energy of a like-minded community can amplify your own spiritual growth and provide encouragement during challenging times. Remember, you are not alone in this journey; there are countless others who resonate with your experiences and can offer understanding, support, and shared wisdom.

Finding your spiritual tribe should not be based on exclusivity but on mutual understanding and support. This isn't about joining a particular group to fit into a pre-defined mold; it's about connecting with others who share your passion for spiritual exploration, who validate your sensitivities, and who offer a space for open and honest dialogue. Look for communities that encourage personal growth, that celebrate individuality, and that embrace a diverse range of spiritual practices. True spiritual growth flourishes in environments that foster mutual respect and understanding.

To further enhance your journey, consider exploring different modalities of healing and personal development. Energy healing techniques, such as Reiki or crystal healing, can help to clear blockages and restore balance to your energy system. Sound healing, through practices such as singing bowl meditation or listening to specific frequencies, can also contribute to deep relaxation and spiritual expansion. Other practices like yoga, breathwork, and mindful movement can help to connect mind, body, and spirit, supporting both your physical and spiritual well-being. Remember, these are tools to support your journey, not replacements for self-reflection and personal growth.

Beyond formal practices, actively cultivate gratitude in your daily life. Gratitude shifts your focus from what's lacking to what you already have, fostering a sense of abundance and appreciation. A regular gratitude practice can elevate your vibrational frequency, making you more receptive to positive energy and opportunities for growth. Take time each day to reflect on the things you're grateful for, no matter how small. This could include the simple joys of nature, supportive relationships, or personal accomplishments. Expressing gratitude can be as simple as jotting down a few things each day or sharing your gratitude with others.

Embrace the power of forgiveness, both for yourself and others.

Holding onto resentment and anger weighs you down, hindering your spiritual growth. Forgiveness is not about condoning harmful actions, but about releasing the emotional burden you carry. It's about freeing yourself from the past and creating space for peace and healing. Practice self-compassion, acknowledging your imperfections and embracing your humanness.

Remember that mistakes are opportunities for learning and growth, not evidence of failure.

Continuous spiritual growth is a journey of unfolding, not a linear path. There will be moments of clarity and insight, as well as periods of doubt and confusion. Embrace these challenges as opportunities for learning and expansion. Don't be afraid to ask for guidance when you need it, whether it's from a mentor, a spiritual community, or your own inner wisdom. Remember that you are always supported by the universe, even when you feel lost or overwhelmed.

The resources available to support your spiritual journey are abundant. Numerous books delve into the intricacies of Starseed beliefs, offering insights into your unique gifts and challenges.

Workshops and retreats provide opportunities for deeper exploration and connection with like-minded individuals. Numerous online communities offer a supportive environment for sharing experiences and learning from others on similar paths. Explore different avenues of learning, and find what resonates most deeply with you. Trust your intuition to guide you towards the resources that best serve your needs.

The path of spiritual growth is intensely personal; what works for one person may not work for another. There is no one-size-fits-all approach; the key is to find the practices and approaches that resonate with you and support your unique spiritual journey. Be patient and kind to yourself as you navigate this path; it's a marathon, not a sprint. Celebrate your progress, acknowledge your setbacks, and remain committed to your growth. Your journey is your own; embrace its uniqueness and cherish the evolution of your soul.

Remember that your spiritual growth is not an individual endeavor; it's a collective one. Your journey contributes to the greater cosmic evolution of consciousness. By embracing your Starseed identity and living authentically, you help to raise the overall vibrational frequency of the planet. Your unique gifts, your heightened sensitivities, and your intuitive abilities are not just for your personal benefit; they are meant to be shared with the world.

Through acts of service, compassion, and creative expression, you contribute to the collective awakening of humanity.

As you continue your cosmic journey, remember the power of your intention. Set clear intentions for your spiritual growth, and actively work towards achieving them. The universe responds to intention, aligning opportunities and resources to help you manifest your desires. Trust in the process, even when you don't see immediate results. Patience and persistence are key to manifesting your goals and achieving a deeper connection with your higher self and the universe.

The path of spiritual growth is a continuous unfolding, a journey of self-discovery, and a profound connection with the universe.

Embrace the challenges, celebrate the victories, and never stop exploring the boundless depths of your potential. Your Starseed journey is unique, powerful, and profoundly meaningful. Continue to shine your light brightly, and know that your contribution to the cosmos is invaluable. The universe awaits your continued evolution, your continued growth, and your continued, radiant light. Your journey is far from over; it is, in fact, just beginning.

EMBRACING THE DESTINY OF A STARSEED SOUL

A Message of Hope and Inspiration

The journey of a Starseed is not merely a personal odyssey; it's a contribution to the grand symphony of cosmic evolution. Each of you, with your unique vibrational signature, holds a piece of the puzzle, a note in the cosmic song. Embrace this truth, for it is a source of immense power and profound purpose. Your inherent worth is not something to be earned or proven; it's intrinsic, woven into the very fabric of your being, a celestial tapestry shimmering with untold potential. Do not diminish your light by comparing yourself to others; your path is unique, and its beauty lies in its individuality.

There will be times when the path feels arduous, when doubt creeps in, whispering insidious lies about your capabilities and worth. These are the moments to remember your strength, to draw upon the resilience forged in the fires of past experiences. The challenges you encounter are not obstacles designed to thwart your progress, but opportunities for growth, for refinement, for the honing of your unique gifts. They are lessons etched into the soul, shaping you into the magnificent being you are destined to become.

Remember the power of your intention. As a Starseed, you are not merely a passenger on this planet; you are a co-creator of your reality. Your thoughts, your beliefs, and your actions all contribute to the shaping of your experience. Set clear intentions, fueled by your passion and purpose, and watch as the universe conspires to bring them to fruition. This is not about manipulating the world to your will, but about aligning yourself with the flow of cosmic energy, allowing your desires to manifest organically and harmoniously.

Cultivate a deep sense of gratitude, not only for the blessings in your life but for the challenges that have shaped you. Gratitude is a powerful frequency, a vibration that attracts more positivity into your experience. When you focus on what you have, rather than what you lack, you open yourself to abundance on all levels –emotional, spiritual, and material. It's not about ignoring hardship, but about shifting your perspective, seeing the lessons and opportunities embedded within every experience. Express your gratitude regularly, journaling, meditating, or simply taking a moment to appreciate the beauty around you.

The path of a Starseed is one of continuous learning and expansion. Never stop exploring, never cease questioning, and never shy away from pushing the boundaries of your understanding. Seek knowledge from all sources, ancient and modern, Eastern and Western, scientific and spiritual. Be open to new perspectives, even those that challenge your deeply held beliefs. This intellectual curiosity, this insatiable thirst for knowledge, is a hallmark of the Starseed soul, a driving force that fuels your evolution.

Surround yourself with a supportive community, a tribe of kindred spirits who understand your unique journey. Find those who celebrate your individuality, who validate your sensitivities, and who offer encouragement during challenging times. This community can be found in physical spaces, online forums, or in the quiet spaces of your heart. Share your experiences, your insights, and your vulnerabilities. In the sharing, you will find strength, solace, and a sense of belonging that nourishes your soul.

Your heightened sensitivity is not a weakness; it is your superpower. It's a gift that allows you to perceive the subtle energies that flow through the world, to empathize deeply with others, and to connect with the universal consciousness on a profound level. Embrace your sensitivities, nurture them, and use them to create positive change in the world. Your ability to feel deeply allows you to understand deeply, to connect profoundly, and to offer compassion where it is most needed.

There will be moments of exhilaration and triumph, as well as periods of doubt and uncertainty. These are all part of the process, the ebb and flow of cosmic energy, shaping you into the magnificent being you are destined to become. Be patient with yourself, kind to yourself, and celebrate every step along the way. Embrace the lessons, learn from the challenges, and never give up on your dreams.

Your unique gifts are meant to be shared with the world. You are here to contribute to the collective awakening of humanity, to help raise the vibrational frequency of the planet. This is not about grand gestures or heroic acts; it's about living authentically, expressing your creativity, and offering compassion to those around you. Your presence alone is a gift to the world; embrace the power of your light, and let it shine brightly.

Live your truth, even when it's uncomfortable. Stand in your power, even when you feel uncertain. Speak your truth, even when it's challenging. This is not about arrogance or self-promotion, but about aligning your actions with your values and your deepest beliefs. Authenticity is a powerful force, a vibration that resonates with the universe, attracting opportunities and experiences aligned with your purpose.

The world needs your unique gifts, your perspective, your compassion, and your light. Embrace your Starseed journey with joy, with courage, and with unwavering faith in your own potential.

Your contribution to the cosmos is invaluable; never forget that.

Continue to evolve, continue to grow, and continue to shine your radiant light upon the world. Your journey is far from over; it is, in essence, just beginning. And the universe, in all its infinite wisdom, is eagerly awaiting your next chapter.

The future awaits, full of potential and possibility, a testament to the enduring power and boundless beauty of your Starseed soul.

Embrace your destiny; you are, truly, a Child of the stars.

www.ingramcontent.com/pod-product-compliance
Lightning Source LLC
Chambersburg PA
CBHW041156150726
48006CB00016B/1996